Calendar Kids

Handprint Quilts through the Year

Marcia L. Layton

Credits

President · *Nancy J. Martin*
CEO · *Daniel J. Martin*
COO · *Tom Wierzbicki*
Publisher · *Jane Hamada*
Editorial Director · *Mary V. Green*
Managing Editor · *Tina Cook*
Technical Editor · *Laurie Baker*
Copy Editor · *Durby Peterson*
Design Director · *Stan Green*
Illustrator · *Laurel Strand*
Cover and Text Designer · *Trina Craig*
Photographer · *Brent Kane*

Calendar Kids: Handprint Quilts through the Year
© 2007 by Marcia L. Layton

That Patchwork Place® is an imprint of Martingale & Company®.

Martingale & Company
20205 144th Ave. NE
Woodinville, WA 98072-8478 USA
www.martingale-pub.com

Printed in China
12 11 10 09 08 07   8 7 6 5 4 3 2 1

Mission Statement

Dedicated to providing quality products and service to inspire creativity.

Library of Congress Cataloging-in-Publication Data
Library of Congress Control Number: 2006026556

ISBN: 978-1-56477-702-7

Dedication

This book is dedicated to my family: my parents, Annie and Fred Stumme; my children, Melissa, Tommy, Robert, and Carrie; and my husband, Steve. Their love, encouragement, patience, and wonderful help made it possible for me to write this book.

Acknowledgments

I would like to thank the following people:

All the children of Play Haven Preschool in Tampa, Florida, who have eagerly lent their little hands to my quilts over the years. With special thanks to my 2004–2005 class of four-year-olds, who fit the term *calendar kids* to perfection, not only because there were twelve of them but also because of their spontaneous and frequently very loud rendition of a song about the months of the year.

My friends and co-teachers, Betsy White, Sue Johnston, Sue Gandy, and my dear friend, Suzanne Crosby, for their wonderful support and encouragement.

My favorite quilt teacher, Florinda Clark, and quilting friends Johnnie Fernandez, Pat Brady, Jo Kolwak and Joy DiMarco for their helpful ideas and fun quilting times.

Michele Heitlinger, who first encouraged me to make a calendar quilt.

The wonderful Martingale & Company staff who have given me this opportunity to share my ideas and who worked so hard to create this book.

CONTENTS

INTRODUCTION

When I started making handprint quilts about eight years ago, I never imagined that I would still find myself busily printing and creating these quilts today. You, too, might wonder what I find to interest me in such simple quilts. "Just how far can you go with a handprint?" and "Why make a quilt with handprints?" are two questions you might ask. From my experiences over the years, I would reply that you can make a handprint into almost anything. And as for the why, well, it's just plain fun, not to mention that a handprint quilt makes a delightful, one-of-a-kind keepsake.

As a preschool teacher, I have had many opportunities to work with young children's handprints. I often paint children's hands and print them on paper for classroom crafts. It's a fun activity for everyone. The real fun doesn't begin, however, until you start to print on fabric.

My first handprint quilt was a simple one, covered with the painted hands of the children in

my class. The handprints were plain, but they were bright and colorful, and the quilt was a lovely memento of the school year. With my second quilt, I started to experiment with the handprints. They were no longer just prints of hands—instead, they took on new identities as flowers and bugs in a quilted garden. As I started looking through favorite fabrics and adding to my collection, ideas for other handprint "creatures" started to form. Soon I was making quilts with handprint fish, dinosaurs, jungle animals, chickens, and more. I would go to bed and wake up with handprint animal quilts in my head! Many of these quilt designs appeared in my book *Handprint Quilts: Creating Children's Keepsakes with Paint and Fabric,* published by Martingale & Company in 2003.

Not content to end my handprint adventure at that point, I started thinking about designs that could be displayed at special times during the year. Like so many other people, I enjoy decorating for the holidays. What could be more fun and precious than a seasonal quilt or pillow made with children's handprints! With that thought, the idea for this book was begun.

The first part of this book details the supplies needed and the process of printing with hands on fabric. It also gives suggestions for embellishing handprints in a variety of ways. The suggestions truly are just suggestions. I've found that with all the wonderful paints and trims available, there are many delightful ways to embellish handprints. The wide variety of fabrics available to the quilter today makes the choice of colors and designs for handprint quilts almost limitless.

The next section contains basic information about constructing and finishing a quilt. All the quilts in this book are perfect for a beginner or the "time-challenged" quilter because the projects are simple and quick to complete. With a little thought and planning, the experienced quilter can easily expand on the designs to make them more intricate and challenging.

Instructions for 14 quilt projects follow the section on quilting basics. The project section opens with "Calendar Kids," a quilt which features twelve unique designs, one for each month of the year. Each of these designs can also be used individually to make small quilts. Following the calendar quilt are projects with designs for the four seasons, all using handprints in a fun and novel way.

The book concludes with a gallery of quilts inspired by the project designs. These quilts differ in color, size, and construction to show the possibilities for even more designs.

Making handprint quilts is a fun and easy way to celebrate the holidays, and the quilts make wonderful keepsakes for friends and family to enjoy for years to come. I hope that after reading this book you'll be tempted to try your "hand" at making many of them!

CREATING A HANDPRINT QUILT

SUPPLIES

Fabric. Use good-quality white or unbleached muslin for the printed areas. Wash and iron it smooth before printing. For the rest of the quilt, you can combine the fabrics of your choice. There are many delightful novelty prints available that can inspire a special theme that's reflected in your handprint design. For quilts that are primarily decorative, you can successfully combine cottons, cotton blends, and synthetics. The simplicity of the quilts makes it possible to use different kinds of fabrics.

This is just a sampling of the wide range of fabric patterns that you can combine with your handprint pieces.

Rotary cutter, ruler, and mat. You will use these for cutting out the pieces to make the quilt blocks, sashings, and borders.

Scissors. You'll need scissors to cut ribbons and other embellishments.

Water-based acrylic craft paints. These paints come in many colors and brands, and you can easily mix them to create additional colors. There are many different paints designated for crafting, but unless they are specifically labeled as fabric paint, they will need to be mixed with fabric medium to be used on a quilt.

Fabric or textile medium. This liquid is usually found in craft stores right next to the acrylic paints. You can mix it with regular acrylic paint to transform the acrylic paint into fabric paint.

Craft brushes. You will use these to paint the children's hands, and you'll need several different sizes. Inexpensive brushes like those used for children's poster paints and watercolors work well.

Paper towels or moistened wipes. Use these for wiping paint off hands.

Containers for mixing paint. I use empty Styrofoam egg cartons, trays, and even paper plates to hold my paint.

Cardboard or heavy paper. This is to put under your fabric as you create your handprints. I like to use cut-up brown grocery bags or pieces of cardboard. You can then tape the fabric to the paper. You will also need a small piece of plastic wrap or a cut-up plastic bag to slip between the fabric and paper to keep the paint from sticking as it dries.

Masking tape. This is used to secure fabric squares to a surface before printing.

Fabric glues. Special glues are available for attaching ribbon, fringes, and other trims to the quilt. Other glues are made especially for attaching googly eyes, beads, gemstones, and other materials.

Fusible web. Use this paper-backed, iron-on webbing to fuse appliqués to the quilt.

Seam sealant. This is important for preventing fraying on the ends of ribbons and cut areas of trim that are not turned under.

Embellishments. You can use embroidery floss, decorative threads, ribbons, rickrack, fringe, sequins, bells, googly eyes, dimensional paint, glitter, and fabric markers to decorate your quilt.

Thread. You will need mercerized cotton or cotton-polyester thread for quilt construction and machine quilting. You can also use invisible nylon thread for machine quilting. Use hand-quilting thread for hand-quilted areas.

Pins. You'll need long quilter's pins and #2 rust-proof safety pins to pin baste your quilt for sewing and quilting.

Assorted hand-sewing needles, a thimble, and an embroidery hoop. You'll need these for making embroidery stitches, attaching beads and sequins, and hand quilting.

Sewing machine. You don't need a fancy sewing machine for these quilts. Any model with a good straight stitch will do.

Assorted sewing machine feet. A foot that measures exactly ¼" from the center needle position to the edge of the foot makes accurate piecing easy. I recommend a walking foot for straight-line quilting.

Low-loft polyester or cotton batting. It's best to use low-loft batting for both hand and machine quilting.

PRINTING THE QUILT

Printing a handprint quilt is not a difficult process, but it does involve some advance preparation and planning. Along with a willing handprint artist, you will need a flat, protected work surface and access to a sink to wash the paint off afterward. Keep a supply of paper towels or moistened wipes nearby.

To begin printing, you will need muslin fabric that has been washed and ironed flat. This should be cut or torn to the desired size of your finished square or panel plus two inches. (The extra inches allow you to trim the piece and nicely center your design after printing.) Before you actually paint, it helps to practice placing the printer's hand on the fabric to decide exactly where you want the handprint to be. You will need to show young children exactly how you want them to put their fingers down, whether spread apart or held together. Practice this a few times. Urge them to let you move their hand and not to move a finger until so directed.

Start by taping the fabric to a piece of heavy paper or cardboard for support. Remember to slip a little piece of plastic wrap or a cut-up plastic bag between the fabric and paper to prevent the paint from sticking as it dries. Set this prepared fabric aside.

Pour a small amount of paint into a small container. If you need to mix colors to get the exact shade you need for your print, you can do that here. Then add about an equal amount of fabric medium to your paint. (Don't make your paint too thin; just aim for a nice painting consistency. You don't want it to drip off the child's hands.)

For some handprints, you will use just one color. (I recommend this especially when you are printing with very young children.) At other times, you might choose to combine several colors in a print. In those cases, have all your paints for the handprint ready at one time. You can carefully paint each section of the hand the desired color and print in one motion. For some prints with small spots or stripes or blended colors, you can apply a base color and then just dab the other colors on top before printing.

Once your paint is ready, work over a covered area (to catch drips and splatters, I usually lay several paper towels underneath the hand I'm painting) and fill your brush with paint. Holding the printer's hand palm side up, paint the hand as desired. Work quickly and cover all areas with an even coat of paint. The painting tickles, so you will probably hear a few giggles from your handprint artist.

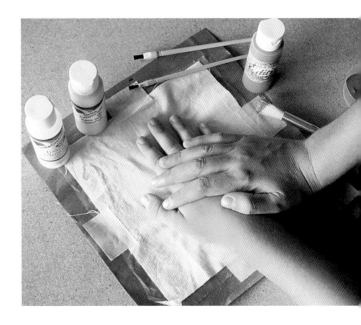

Next, carefully lift the hand. Sometimes the fabric will try to pull up as well. The tape will help keep it in place, but you will probably also have to pull the fabric down. Again, be careful not to accidentally touch any paint from your hands to the fabric.

To avoid having paint end up where you don't want it, paint only one hand at a time. Immediately after printing, send your printer straight to the sink to wash up. With young children, it's best to hold their wrist all the way to the sink and help them wash!

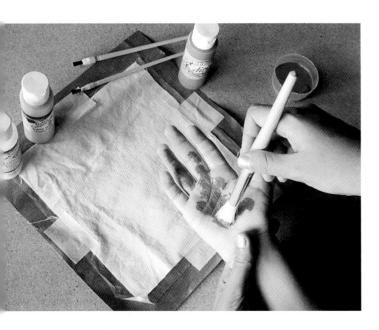

Now carefully move over to your piece of fabric, turn the hand over, and place it where desired. Press each finger from the tip toward the palm and at each joint. Press down firmly on the printer's palm. (You usually get some paint on your own hands while doing this, so be careful not to get it on the fabric.)

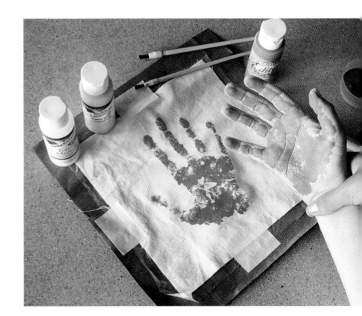

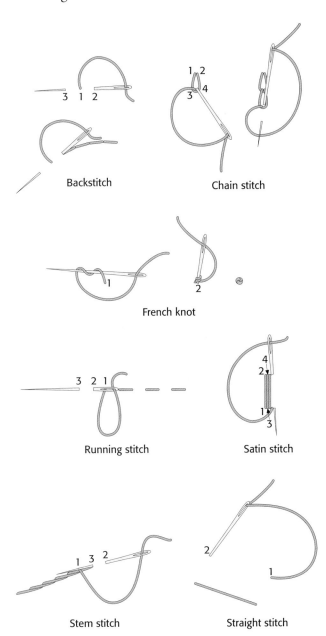

Set the handprint aside to dry. The paint will be dry to the touch in less than an hour.

Remove the tape and lift the fabric from the paper and plastic to allow it to finish drying. It will later need to be heat-set with an iron. The brand of textile medium that you use will determine the length of time to wait before heat-setting and ironing. Follow the instructions for your particular brand to heat-set the print and press the block.

If desired, use a permanent-ink fabric pen to write the name of the handprint artist on the block.

EMBELLISHING THE QUILT

After your printing is done and the handprints have dried and been heat-set, trim the printed piece to the desired size, centering the print nicely. You are now ready to start embellishing your print. Most of the embellishment is done before the quilt top is constructed, unless a particular embellishment will be too close to a seam line and could interfere with later sewing and machine quilting.

When embellishing your prints, you are limited only by your imagination and the materials you have available. Embroidery is a wonderful way to create handprint features. It is best worked in a hoop, taking care not to pull too hard on the painted print to avoid distorting it. I use a size 7 embroidery needle when working with three strands of floss and a size 22 chenille needle for six strands of floss and ribbon floss.

It can be difficult to pull thread through thicker areas of paint, so a thimble will come in handy at times. It is also important to plan carefully where you will embroider, because the paint does not forgive mistakes very well. If you have to rip out stitches, needle holes will show.

The following embroidery stitches are used for the designs shown in this book.

Backstitch

Chain stitch

French knot

Running stitch

Satin stitch

Stem stitch

Straight stitch

Sequins and beads are additional embellishments that I use to add sparkle to my quilts. They're easy to attach using a needle that is thin enough to pass through the bead, and all-purpose thread in a color to match the bead or sequin. I find that a size 10 milliner's needle works well for both beads and sequins. To apply beads, just stitch them in place where you want them. Some can even be glued in place. To apply sequins, I bring the needle and thread up in the fabric where I want to place the sequin, thread a sequin and a matching-color seed bead onto the needle, and then pass the needle back through the sequin hole. If there isn't too much distance between sequins, you can continue to add them in this manner, securing the last one with a knot.

Attaching sequins

Using dimensional fabric paint is another fun way to bring handprints to life. This paint comes in many bright and glittery colors and can create interesting designs and textures on the prints. You can use fabric markers to personalize handprints and to add features as well.

To add even more interest to handprints, you can use permanent glues to attach trims to your quilt. Bells, braids, buttons, googly eyes, feathers, fringes, fusible appliqués, ribbons, and tiny resin figures are all items that I have used successfully. Finding the perfect accessories to complete these quilts is half the fun!

You can wash your printed quilt as long as the embellishments you use are washable. For best results, limit the embellishments to embroidery, buttons, fabric trims, or dimensional paint if the quilt is to be laundered. Anything secured with fabric glue might come unglued during washing, depending on the type of glue you use. Be sure to stitch trims in place.

Note: *When making quilts for young children, limit embellishments to embroidery or dimensional paint. Other small embellishments could pose a choking hazard.*

CONSTRUCTING AND FINISHING THE QUILT

After the handprints have been printed and embellished, you're ready to assemble your quilt top. Using ¼" seam allowances, sew sashing and borders to the muslin handprint blocks and panels. Refer to "Adding Borders" on page 11 to add butted-corner borders to your quilt. Then finish the quilt with either binding or rickrack edging as described on pages 11–13.

Adding Borders

The quilts in this book all have simple butted-corner borders. The lengths of the border strips are listed in the cutting instructions for each project. However, if the quilt top has many seams, you may wish to measure the actual top before cutting the border strips to ensure that the strips will fit the quilt. Stretching can occur during construction, causing the edges of the quilt top to measure longer than the length through the center of the quilt, and seam allowances sewn wider than ¼" can cause a quilt top to "shrink." If you decide to measure your quilt top, do it through the center in both directions and cut the border strips to the measured lengths. You can cut border strips on the crosswise grain of the fabric and piece them to be as long as necessary. I choose not to piece my borders; therefore, I have to cut the longer border strips from the lengthwise grain of the fabric. Lengthwise-grain strips are also necessary when working with directional prints.

Finishing with Binding

Make a quilt sandwich by layering the backing (right side down, taped to a flat, smooth surface), the batting, and the quilt top (right side up). Pin baste the layers of fabric and batting together using #2 rustproof safety pins spaced every 6" to 8" throughout the quilt; then remove the tape.

With a walking foot on your sewing machine, quilt by stitching in the ditch along the seam line around each handprint square or panel, working from the center of the quilt out toward the edges. Follow the quilting instructions given for each project to add further quilting to your handprint quilt. After quilting, trim the batting and backing even with the edges of the quilt top.

Bind the quilt with French double-fold binding, cutting 2"-wide binding strips across the width of the fabric. Sew the binding strips together, placing them right sides together and at right angles as shown, to equal the measurement of the perimeter of the quilt plus 10". Trim ¼" from the stitching and press the seam allowances open.

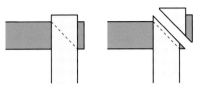

Joining straight-cut strips

Press the strips in half lengthwise with the wrong sides together. After preparing your binding strips, you may bind the quilt with a simple straight binding, which is cut to fit the sides of the quilt and has overlapped corners, or with a continuous binding, which has mitered corners. I use the two bindings interchangeably.

For overlapped corners:

1. Measure the quilt top vertically through the center and cut two binding strips to that measurement. Fold the strips in half lengthwise, wrong sides together, and press. Pin-mark the center of the quilt top along the side edges and pin-mark the centers of the binding strips. Pin the binding strips to the front of the quilt top along the side edges, matching pin marks and ends. Sew in place using a ¼" seam allowance. Fold the binding to the back of the quilt and blindstitch in place, just covering the stitching line.

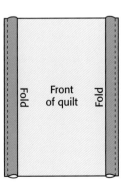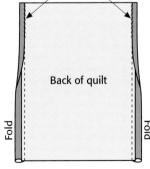

Match raw edges.

2. Measure the quilt top horizontally through the center and cut two binding strips to that measurement plus 1". Fold the strips in half lengthwise, wrong sides together, and press. Pin-mark the center of the quilt top along the top and bottom edges and pin-mark the centers of the binding strips. Pin the binding strips to the front of the quilt top along the top and bottom edges, matching pin marks and allowing the binding to extend ½" beyond each end. Sew in place, using a ¼" seam allowance. Fold in the ends; then fold the binding to the back of the quilt and blindstitch in place, just covering the stitching line.

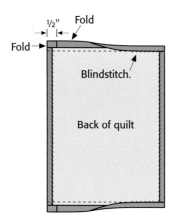

For mitered corners:

1. Temporarily position the binding around the quilt, matching up the raw edges and making sure that none of the seams fall at the corners of the quilt. Leaving an 8" tail at the beginning, pin and then sew the binding in place along one side using a ¼" seam allowance.

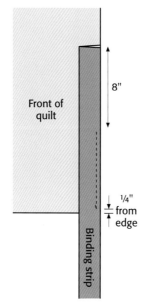

2. Stop ¼" away from the corner, backstitch, and remove the quilt from the machine. Rotate the quilt 90° and position it so that you will be stitching down the next side. Fold the binding up, away from the quilt, creasing it at a 45° angle. Fold the strip back down on itself so that it is parallel with the edge of the quilt. The fold should be even with the top edge of the quilt.

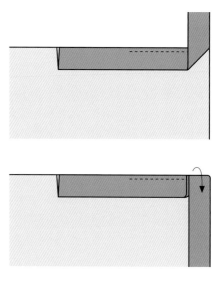

3. Begin stitching at the top edge and continue down the side of the quilt.

4. Repeat steps 2 and 3 at each corner. Stop stitching about 8" away from where you began stitching. Backstitch and remove the quilt from the machine. Trim the binding so that the tails overlap 2" (or the width of your binding).

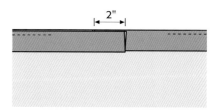

5. Open up the strips and place them right sides together at right angles. Stitch on the diagonal as shown.

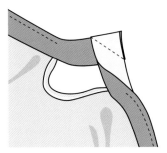

6. Trim the seam to ¼" and press open. Refold the binding and finish sewing it to the quilt.

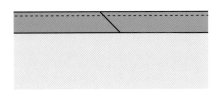

7. To finish the binding, fold the binding to the back of the quilt and blindstitch in place. A miter will form at each corner. Blindstitch the miter.

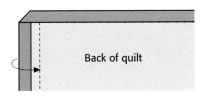

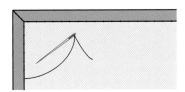

Finishing with Rickrack Edging

Before you make your quilt sandwich (backing, batting, and quilt top), sew the rickrack along the edge of the quilt top, centering the trim ¼" from the raw edges. (This is exactly where your seam line will fall when you sew your quilt together.) It's easier to cut a separate piece of trim for each side than to go around the corners with one long piece. For neat corners, make sure that the rickrack tapers off (ends with a valley rather than a hump) at the corners.

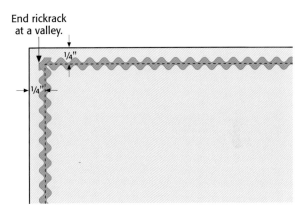

Center and sew rickrack ¼" from raw edges.

Layer the quilt with the batting first, the backing fabric (right side up) next, and then the quilt top (right side down). Pin together along the edges. Stitch ¼" from the outer edges using the stitching line from the rickrack as a guide, and leave an opening about 18" long on one edge. Turn the quilt right side out through the opening and slipstitch the opening closed.

Pin baste the layers of fabric and batting together with rustproof safety pins, spacing the pins 6" to 8" apart. With a walking foot on your sewing machine, quilt by stitching in the ditch along the seam line around each handprint square or panel, working from the center of the quilt out toward the edges. Add further quilting to your handprint quilt by following any additional quilting instructions given for your project.

Attaching a Hanging Sleeve

Cut a 9"-wide strip of fabric equal to the width of the quilt top minus 2". Press each end under ¼". Press under ¼" again and stitch along the folded edges.

To attach a hanging sleeve to a quilt that will be bound:

1. Fold the sleeve strip in half lengthwise, wrong sides together, and press.

2. Center the sleeve on the back of the quilt at the upper edge. Line up the raw edges of the sleeve with the raw edge of the quilt sandwich. Pin in place and machine baste along the raw edges. The top edge will be further secured when the binding is attached.

3. Bind the quilt.

4. After binding, blindstitch the bottom of the sleeve and the bottom layer of fabric at the sleeve ends to the back of the quilt.

To attach a hanging sleeve to a quilt with rickrack edging:

1. Apply the rickrack to the quilt as described in "Finishing with Rickrack Edging" on page 13.

2. Fold the sleeve strip in half lengthwise, wrong sides together. Sew the long edges together to form a tube. Center the seam in the back of the sleeve and press it open.

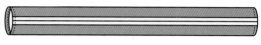

Press seam open.

3. Sew the sleeve to the back of the quilt just below the top edge of the quilt, with the sleeve seam against the quilt back. Blindstitch the sleeve in place along the top and bottom edges and blindstitch the bottom layer of fabric at each end.

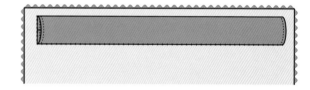

Labeling the Quilt

For a finishing touch, add a quilt label to the back of your quilt with your name, the date, the place, and any other special information about the quilt. Be sure to include the names of your handprint artists and their ages, if they are children. Photo labels are especially nice when the quilt is made for a school group. To make a simple label, write the desired information on a small rectangle of fabric using a permanent-ink pen. Turn under the raw edges and blindstitch the label to the back of your quilt.

TIPS FOR PLANNING YOUR OWN QUILT

Each quilt in this book is as unique as the hands that printed it. When you plan your own handprint quilt, you'll need to consider many things, such as the number of hands you are printing, the age of your handprint artist(s), and the size you want your finished quilt to be. Other factors, such as the fabrics you want to use, the trims available, and your personal preferences, will also affect your planning decisions.

When I plan a handprint quilt, I first consider the number and size of hands I am printing. Most of my quilts are used as decorative wall hangings, so the finished quilt size is a factor too. For a single block, I will look at the largest handprint, decide how much white background is desirable, and set my block size from that measurement. If I am printing a number of hands that can be displayed in even rows, I usually decide to proceed with even rows of individual blocks that are set apart with sashing. However, if I am printing a large number of hands that would result in a very large quilt if printed individually, I will print panels where the handprints can be placed closer together. Panels also work well if the number of handprints is uneven. The only drawback to panels is that you must take extra care while printing, because one misprint can ruin the whole panel.

The age of your artist is another important consideration when you're planning the complexity of the prints. Single, one-color prints work best for very young children. Children this age usually don't have the patience or control for extensive painting and exact positioning of their hands. They do enjoy the process, however.

Once you decide how you wish to print the hands, you'll need to assemble your border fabrics and some of the trims to complete your design. Your own preferences and the availability of these items are the guiding factors. Because most of these quilts are not designed to be washable, you can get creative in your choices of fabrics and trims. Your choices will in turn influence the selection of colors for the handprints.

Each quilt design in this book is different because of one or more of the considerations mentioned here. Each design can be enlarged or reduced simply by adding blocks or adjusting the block size and then adjusting the borders using some simple math. As you look through each quilt project, you'll find that I've included notes and suggestions for altering the look and making each design your own. Have fun hand printing!

Calendar Kids

By Marcia L. Layton. Printed by the 2003–2004 class of 4-year-olds at Play Haven Preschool.

This colorful quilt offers a handprint design for each month of the year.

FINISHED QUILT: 56½" x 72¾"
FINISHED BLOCK: 15" x 15"

MATERIALS

Yardage is based on 42"-wide fabric.

- ¼ yard *each* of 12 theme prints for Handprint block inner borders and 12 coordinating fabrics for Handprint block outer borders (1 inner-border and 1 outer-border fabric for *each* block)
- 2⅛ yards of black-and-white print for outer border and binding
- 2 yards of black solid for sashing and inner border
- 1½ yards of white muslin for Handprint blocks
- 3¾ yards of fabric for quilt backing
- 61" x 77" piece of batting
- 8 yards of black piping
- **Acrylic paints:** blue for mittens, ladybug, and fireworks; red for heart, flower, fireworks, and apple; green for shamrock, flower, and Christmas tree; yellow for Easter basket, flower, and leaf; aqua for Easter basket and flip-flops; pink for flower; orange for flower, jack-o'-lantern, and leaf; white for fireworks; and black for jack-o'-lantern
- **Embroidery floss:** blue for mittens, light green and golden yellow for Easter basket, black for flower and jack-o'-lantern, red for flower and flip-flops, and brown for apple and leaf
- **Sequins:** 2 iridescent snowflakes and 14 iridescent 8-mm round for mittens; 6 black 5-mm round, 7 black 8-mm round, and 2 black 12-mm round for ladybug; 30 each of red, silver, and blue 5-mm stars for fireworks; 14 gold 5-mm stars, 6 blue 5-mm round, 6 red 8-mm round, 1 gold 12-mm star, and 10 iridescent snowflakes for Christmas tree
- Glass 10/0 seed beads in amount and colors to match sequins
- **Buttons:** 16 assorted pink and red for heart, 2 suns for flip-flops, 2 acorns and 2 leaves for leaf
- **Baby rickrack:** ⅔ yard of red for heart, 1½ yards of gold metallic for shamrock
- Wire "Love" decoration for heart
- **Medium rickrack:** ½ yard *each* of yellow and gold for Easter basket
- **⅜"-wide ribbon:** ½ yard of pink satin for Easter basket, ⅝ yard of green satin for flower, ⅓ yard of red-and-white polka-dot grosgrain for flip-flops, ⅓ yard of green grosgrain for apple, ⅛ yard of brown grosgrain and ⅓ yard of red satin for Christmas tree
- **Ribbon rosettes:** 5 pink for Easter basket
- **Dimensional fabric paints:** black for ladybug and jack-o'-lantern, gold glitter for Christmas tree
- **Googly eyes:** 1 pair of 8-mm for ladybug, 1 pair of 5-mm for apple, and 1 pair of 5-mm for jack-o'-lantern
- **Iron-on appliqués:** 6 assorted-color daisies for ladybug
- Fabric glue
- **Pom-poms:** 1 green ⅜" pom-pom and 4 green ⅛" pom-poms for apple
- **Hand-sewing needles:** size 10 milliner's, size 7 embroidery

All measurements include ¼"-wide seam allowances.	
Fabric	**Pieces to Cut**
White muslin	12 squares, 11½" x 11½"
Each theme print	2 strips, 1¾" x 9½"
	2 strips, 1¾" x 12"
Each coordinating print	2 strips, 2¼" x 12"
	2 strips, 2¼" x 15½"
Black solid (cut on *lengthwise* grain)	2 strips, 1¾" x 64¼"
	2 strips, 1¾" x 50½"
	3 strips, 1¾" x 48"
	8 strips, 1¾" x 15½"
Black-and-white print (cut on *lengthwise* grain)	2 strips, 3½" x 66¾"
	2 strips, 3½" x 56½"
	4 strips, 2½" x 70"

MAKING THE HANDPRINT BLOCKS

With straight pins, mark off the finished size of each muslin square (9" x 9"). Refer to "Printing the Quilt" on page 7 and "Embellishing the Quilt" on page 9. Use the quilt photos that accompany each block as a placement guide for the painted features and embellishments. Use three strands of embroidery floss unless otherwise directed.

January: Mittens

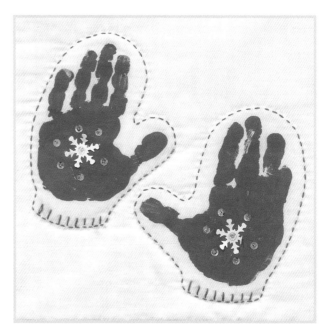

Printed by 4-year-old Lauren Pieper

1. With blue paint, print both right and left hands within a muslin square; print the hands with the fingers together and the thumb extended. Heat-set the handprints.

2. Outline the hands with a running stitch of blue floss to create the shape of mittens, and use long, straight stitches below the hands to make the cuffs.

3. Attach a snowflake sequin to the center of each handprint with a round 8-mm iridescent sequin and matching seed bead. Sew an 8-mm round iridescent sequin and matching seed bead at each point of the snowflake.

February: Heart

Printed by 4-year-old Sarina Hunt

1. Pin-mark the center top and bottom of a muslin square. Use these pins as guides for centering the handprints.

2. With red paint, print the right hand in the vertical center of the square at a 45° angle to the imaginary centerline between the pins, with the fingers and thumb held close together. The fingers should point in toward the center of the square, and the ends of the thumb and middle finger should fall on your imaginary centerline.

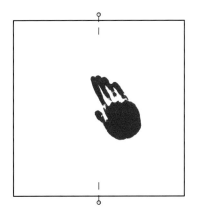

3. Repeat the process with the left hand, printing at the same angle on the other side of the centerline. The tips of the left thumb and middle finger should overlap the fingertips of the right handprint. Heat-set the handprints.

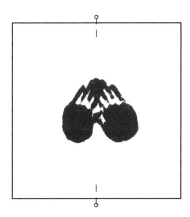

4. Rotate the fabric square so the image is upside down. Glue 16 assorted pink and red buttons to the handprints. These can later be sewn in place for a more secure bond if desired.

5. Glue red baby rickrack around the handprints to emphasize the shape of the heart. Glue the wire "Love" decoration or other embellishment to the background.

March: Shamrock

Printed by 4-year-old Samantha Kaltenbacher

1. With green paint, print a right hand on a muslin square with the fingers spread slightly and the thumb extended. Rotate the square a quarter turn and position another right handprint at a 90° angle to the first print, with the fingers held in a similar position. Rotate the square another quarter turn and make a left handprint. This handprint will be a mirror image of the first one. Heat-set the handprints.

2. Glue gold baby rickrack around the handprints in the shape of a shamrock.

April: Easter Basket

Printed by 4-year-old Grey Young

1. With yellow paint, print the right hand near the lower-right corner of a muslin square with the fingers spread slightly and the thumb extended. Rotate the block so that the handprint is upside down and print the left hand in the lower-left corner of the block with the fingers spread slightly and the thumb extended. The fingers on this hand will fit into the spaces between the fingers of the right handprint.

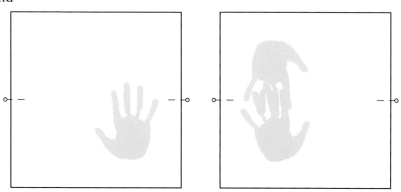

2. Rotate the block so that the two handprints are across the bottom of the square with the thumbs pointing upward. With aqua paint,

make six thumbprints in the area between the yellow thumbprints and just above the fingerprints. Heat-set the prints.

3. Intertwine the yellow and gold medium rickrack for the basket handle; trim to 13". Carefully glue the trim in an arc above the handprints, extending from the bottom of one thumbprint to the bottom of the other.

4. Cut the pink satin ribbon in half and tie each piece into a bow. Glue the bows in place at the ends of the handle; trim the ribbon ends as needed.

5. With light green floss, make long straight stitches in a zigzag pattern, weaving in and out between the aqua thumbprints. With golden yellow floss, make random straight stitches all over the handprints to represent a basket weave.

6. Glue the ribbon rosettes among the aqua thumbprints.

May: Flower

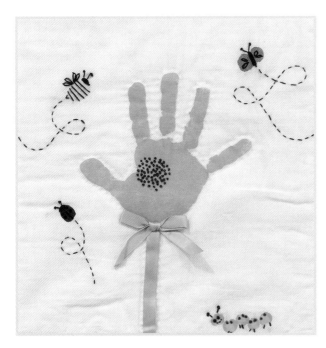

Printed by 4-year-old Laurel Thaxton

1. With the fingers spread, make a pink handprint just above the center of a muslin square.

2. Print fingerprint insects around this center handprint as follows: With an index finger, make a single yellow fingerprint bee and a single red fingerprint ladybug on the left side of the center handprint. To form a butterfly, make two orange fingerprints, side by side and touching each other, on the right side of the handprint. Along the lower-right edge of the block, make a caterpillar by printing five green fingerprints in a row. The prints should be staggered and touching each other. Heat-set the prints.

3. Add the embroidery details to the insects, using black floss for all but the French knots on the worm's body, which are done in red. Stitch approximately 60 red French knots in a circle near the center of the handprint.

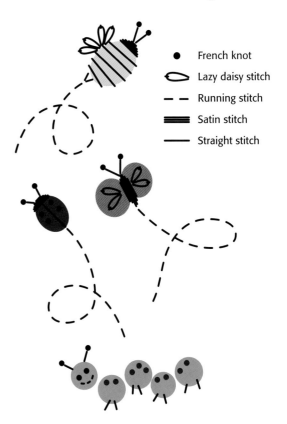

4. Glue a piece of green satin ribbon under the handprint, extending from the base of the hand to the bottom of the square. Tie a bow from the remainder of the ribbon and glue it to the base of the hand; trim the ends as needed.

June: Ladybug

Printed by 4-year-old Trevor Jay

1. With blue paint, print a right hand diagonally across the center of a muslin square. Print the hand with all the fingers held together. Heat-set the handprint. Rotate the square so the fingers are pointing downward.

2. Create an oval head, feelers, and wing detail on the handprint using black dimensional paint.

3. Glue the 8-mm googly eyes to the head. Sew the black 5-mm, 8-mm, and 12-mm sequins onto the ladybug's back with matching seed beads.

4. Iron the fusible flower appliqués onto the background.

July: Fireworks

Printed by 4-year-old Andrew Mathias

1. With the fingers spread, print one red, one white, and one blue handprint on a muslin square so that the palms are almost touching at the square center and the fingers of each handprint are pointing in different directions. Heat-set the prints.

2. Embellish each handprint with 5-mm red, silver, or blue sequin stars and seed beads to match each handprint color.

August: Flip-Flops

Printed by 4-year-old Carlyn Duke

1. With aqua paint, print right and left footprints side by side on the center of a muslin square. Heat-set the footprints.

2. Using red floss and a running stitch, outline the footprints in a flip-flop shape.

3. Cut the red polka-dot ribbon in half. For each flip-flop, pinch a ribbon length together slightly off-center. With matching all-purpose thread, stitch through the ribbon at this point and pull it together tightly. Stitch the pinched portion of the ribbon to the footprint between the big toe and the toe next to it. Tie a knot in each end of the ribbon and glue the ends to the running stitches on each side of the footprint.

4. Sew a decorative sun-shaped button to the footprint where the ribbon is attached between the toes.

September: Apple

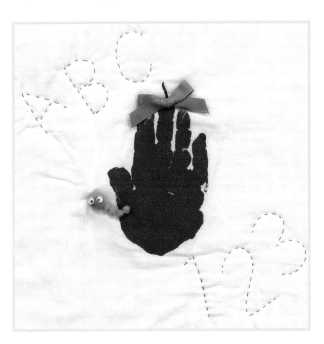

Printed by 4-year-old Corey Khaw

1. With red paint, print a single right hand with the fingers together in the center of the block. Heat-set the print.

2. With brown floss, stem stitch a line that extends about ½" from the top of the handprint for a stem.

3. Glue one ⅜" and four ⅛" green pom-poms to the side of the handprint to form a caterpillar. Glue two 5-mm googly eyes to the large pom-pom.

4. Tie the green grosgrain ribbon into a bow and glue it to the top of the handprint at the base of the stem; trim the ends as needed.

Note: *The letters and numbers will be added during quilting.*

October: Jack-o'-Lantern

Printed by 4-year-old Oliver Ihrig

1. With orange paint, print a right hand in the center of a muslin square, keeping the fingers close together. In the upper-left corner of the block, use black paint to make a single fingerprint for the spider body. Heat-set the prints.

2. Use black dimensional paint to draw a jack-o'-lantern face on the handprint and eight legs on the fingerprint to represent a spider.

3. Use black floss to chain stitch a line from the top of the block to the spider.

4. Glue two 5-mm googly eyes to the spider.

   Note: *The web will be added during quilting.*

November: Leaf

Printed by 4-year-old Skylar McCain

1. Using a mixture of orange and yellow paints, print a right hand, with the three middle fingers held together and the thumb and pinkie extended, onto a muslin square. Heat-set the print.

2. Use brown embroidery floss and a running stitch to stitch veins through the center of the handprint and into the finger areas. With a running stitch, outline the handprint in a leaf shape. If needed, use a real maple leaf as a pattern.

3. Sew the acorn and leaf buttons to the background.

December: Christmas Tree

Printed by 4-year-old Gino Jurado

1. With green paint, print a left hand in the center of a muslin square, keeping the fingers together. Heat-set the print.

2. Cut and glue a 1½" length of brown grosgrain ribbon at the base of the handprint for a tree trunk. Turn under the bottom edge of the ribbon so that it won't fray. Tie the red satin ribbon into a bow and glue it to the top of the brown ribbon where it meets the handprint; trim the ends as needed.

3. With gold glitter dimensional paint, add a garland to the handprint.

4. Embellish the handprint with gold 5-mm star sequins, blue 5-mm round sequins, red 8-mm round sequins, and matching seed beads. Sew a 12-mm gold sequin star and a matching seed bead to the tip of the middle finger.

5. Sew the iridescent snowflake sequins and matching seed beads in a circle around the handprint.

CONSTRUCTING THE QUILT

1. Trim each Handprint block to 9½" x 9½", keeping the design centered.

2. Sew the 1¾" x 9½" theme print strips to the sides of each corresponding block, and then sew the 1¾" x 12" theme print strips to the top and bottom. Press the seam allowances toward the strips after each addition.

3. Sew the 2¼" x 12" coordinating print strips to the sides of each block, and then sew the 2¼" x 15½" coordinating print strips to the top and bottom. Press the seam allowances toward the strips after each addition.

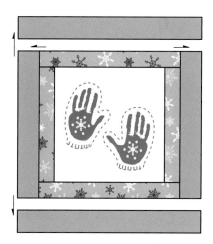

4. Referring to the photo on page 16 for placement, lay out the blocks and 1¾" x 15½" black sashing strips in four rows as shown. Sew the

blocks and strips in each row together. Press the seam allowances toward the sashing.

Make 4.

5. Refer to the quilt assembly diagram to sew the block rows together, inserting a 1¾" x 48" black sashing strip between each row. Press the seam allowances toward the sashing.

6. Sew the 1¾" x 64¼" black inner-border strips to the sides of the quilt, and then sew the 1¾" x 50½" black inner-border strips to the top and bottom. Press the seam allowances toward the border after each addition.

7. Sew the 3½" x 66¾" black-and-white outer-border strips to the sides of the quilt, and then sew the 3½" x 56½" black-and-white outer-border strips to the top and bottom. Press the seam allowances toward the outer border after each addition.

8. Position and pin the piping around the quilt so that the piping stitching line is ¼" from the quilt raw edges and the piping raw edges are facing toward the quilt edges. Sew on the piping stitching line. Snip the seam allowance *of the piping only* close to the stitching at each corner to help it lie flat.

FINISHING THE QUILT

1. Referring to "Finishing with Binding" on page 11, construct the quilt sandwich, pin baste, and machine quilt along the seam lines.

2. Quilt the letters *ABC* and numerals *123* above and below the handprint in the September block. Quilt a spiderweb across the October block. Quilt within each of the remaining blocks. For this quilt, each handprint design was outlined.

3. If desired, refer to "Attaching a Hanging Sleeve" on page 14 to attach a hanging sleeve to the back of the quilt.

4. Use the black-and-white strips to bind the quilt edges.

5. Add a label to the back of the quilt.

The 2003–2004 class of 4-year-olds at Play Haven Preschool in Tampa, Florida

Back row, left to right: Lauren, Trevor, Oliver, Andrew, Samantha, Gino
Front row, left to right: Skylar, Grey, Corey, Sarina, Laurel, Carlyn

Special Design Tips

- Each block in the "Calendar Kids" quilt can become a small seasonal quilt on its own. The blocks can be constructed individually and finished off as small decorative banners to be changed each month as the year progresses.

- The individual blocks can also be repeated in bigger quilts with a single theme. For example, you could make a whole quilt of jack-o'-lanterns, each with a different expression on its face. By varying the colors of the handprints in each block, you can turn designs like the leaves, flowers, bugs, and flip-flops into charming theme quilts.

- If you're printing the hands of older children or adults, it might be wise to use single handprint designs in place of some of the multiple handprint designs to avoid increasing the size of your muslin blocks.

- Many of the other designs in this book could be part of a calendar quilt. For example, you could replace the shamrock for March with a single kite (see "Checkerboard Kites" on page 30), and the basket in April could become an umbrella (see "Umbrella Days" on page 33). July's fireworks and August's flip-flops could be replaced with a flamingo, sea creature, summer berry, or sunshine face.

- You could also create your own handprint designs. Think about things that remind you of each month or season and work them into a handprint. The following photos of other blocks I've created will get you started.

Here's an "egg-citing" substitute for the Easter Basket block. Printed by 4-year-old Reilly Goss.

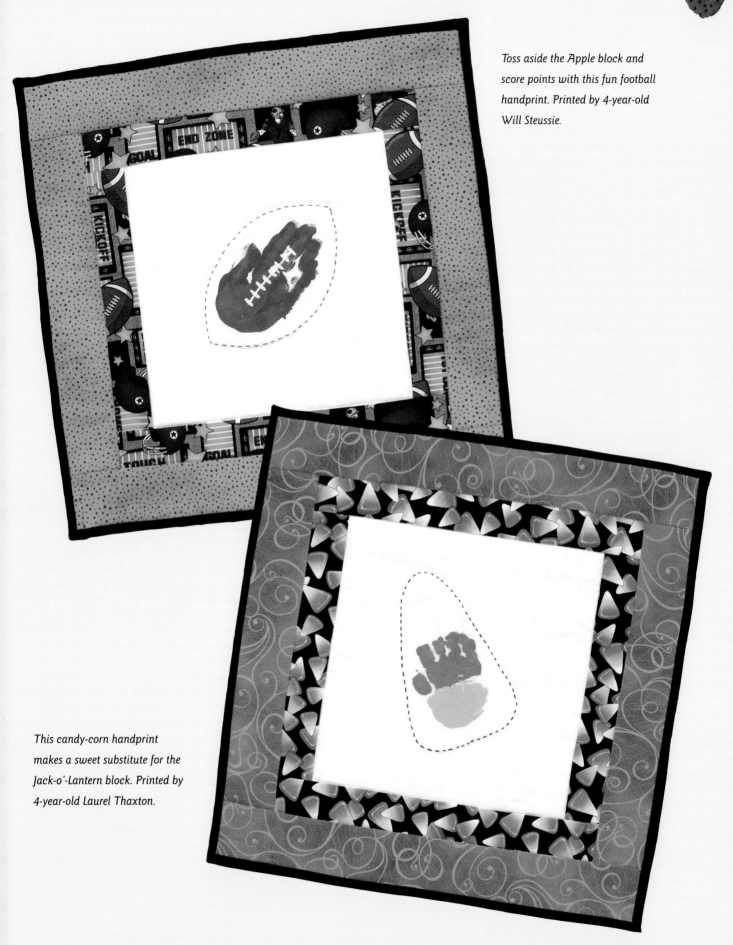

Toss aside the Apple block and score points with this fun football handprint. Printed by 4-year-old Will Steussie.

This candy-corn handprint makes a sweet substitute for the Jack-o'-Lantern block. Printed by 4-year-old Laurel Thaxton.

Checkerboard Kites

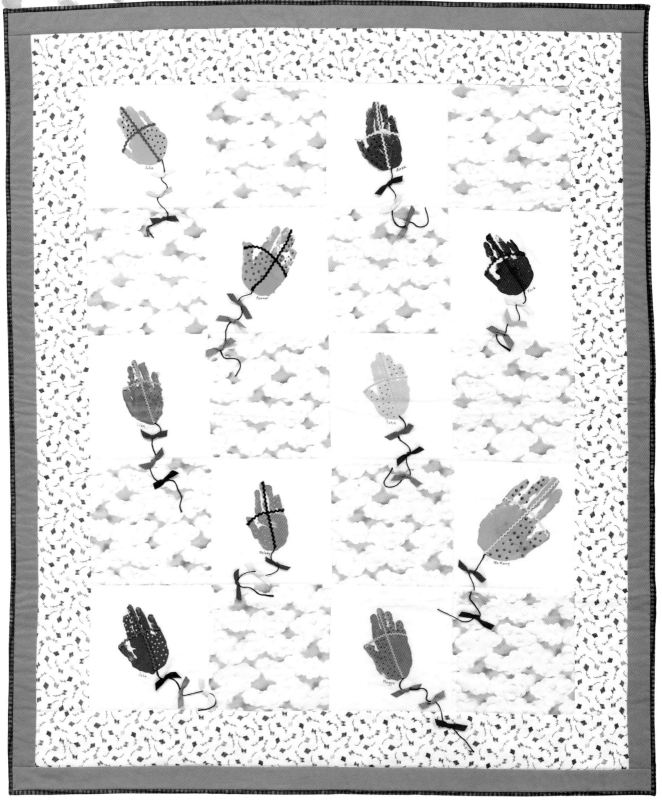

By Marcia L. Layton and the 2004–2005 class of 4-year-olds at Play Haven Preschool.

March winds blow colorful handprint kites across a checkerboard of alternating white and cloud print squares.

Finished quilt: 42½" x 50½"

MATERIALS

Yardage is based on 42"-wide fabric.

- 1½ yards of blue solid for outer border
- 1⅓ yards of white muslin for Handprint blocks
- 1⅓ yards of kite print for inner border
- ⅞ yard of cloud print for alternating blocks
- ⅜ yard of dark blue print for binding
- 2⅞ yards of fabric for backing
- 47" x 55" piece of batting
- **Acrylic paints:** lavender, light green, orange, pink, red, royal blue, yellow, and turquoise
- **Baby rickrack:** ½ yard *each* of blue, light blue, green, light green, orange, pink, purple, red, and yellow
- Fabric glue
- **Dimensional fabric paints:** blue, green, orange, pink, purple, red, yellow, and turquoise
- Black embroidery floss
- **¼"-wide satin or grosgrain ribbon:** ⅓ yard *each* of blue, light blue, fuchsia, green, light green, lavender, orange, pink, bright pink, purple, red, and yellow
- Size 22 chenille needle

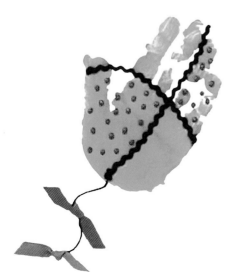

All measurements include ¼"-wide seam allowances.	
Fabric	**Pieces to Cut**
White muslin	10 squares, 10½" x 10½"
Cloud print	10 squares, 8½" x 8½"
Kite print (cut on *lengthwise* grain)	2 strips, 4" x 40½"
	2 strips, 4" x 39½"
Blue solid (cut on *lengthwise* grain)	2 strips, 2" x 47½"
	2 strips, 2" x 42½"
Dark blue print	5 strips, 2" x 42"

MAKING THE HANDPRINT BLOCKS

Refer to "Printing the Quilt" on page 7.

1. With straight pins, mark off the finished size of each muslin square (8" x 8"). With the fingers and thumb held together, print one handprint on each of the muslin squares. Use two of the paint colors twice and the remaining colors once. Heat-set the prints.

2. Glue a piece of baby rickrack down the center length of each handprint and a second piece of the same color across the center width of each print. The rickrack will divide the handprint into quadrants. Using varied colors of dimensional paints, make tiny dots on each handprint in two quadrants that are diagonally across from each other. Allow the paint to dry thoroughly.

3. Cut an 8" length of embroidery floss. Thread all six strands through the chenille needle and tie one end in a knot. Coming up from the back of the square, insert the needle at the bottom of the handprint on one of the muslin squares. Pull the floss through until the knot stops it. Remove the needle from the floss so the floss hangs freely for the kite tail. Repeat with the remaining blocks.

4. Cut each length of ribbon into three equal pieces. Refer to the photo to tie three different-colored pieces onto each kite tail; trim the ends as needed.

5. Trim the Handprint blocks to 8½" x 8½", keeping the tails out of the way and the design centered.

CONSTRUCTING THE QUILT

1. Arrange the Handprint blocks and the alternate Cloud blocks in five rows as shown, alternating the Handprint blocks with the Cloud blocks to form a checkerboard pattern. Sew the blocks in each row together. Press the seam allowances in opposite directions from row to row.

2. Sew the rows together, being careful not to catch the kite tails in the seams. Press the seam allowances in one direction.

3. Sew the 4" x 40½" kite print inner-border strips to the sides of the quilt, and then sew the 4" x 39½" kite print inner-border strips to the top and bottom. Press the seam allowances toward the border after each addition.

4. Sew the 2" x 47½" blue solid outer-border strips to the sides of the quilt, and then sew the 2" x 42½" blue solid outer-border strips to the top and bottom. Press the seam allowances toward the outer border after each addition.

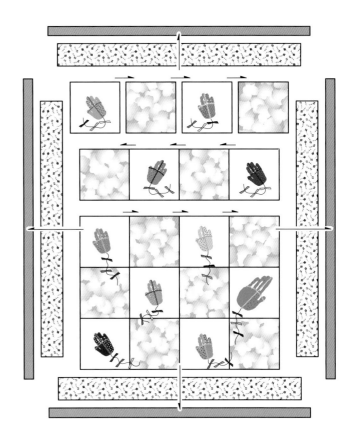

FINISHING THE QUILT

1. Referring to "Finishing with Binding" on page 11, construct the quilt sandwich, pin baste, and machine quilt along the seam lines. Be careful not to catch the kite tails in the stitching.

2. Put a small dot of glue under each ribbon tie and fix the kite tails in place as desired. They can curve around and extend over the seam lines into the Cloud blocks or inner border.

3. If desired, refer to "Attaching a Hanging Sleeve" on page 14 to attach a hanging sleeve to the back of the quilt.

4. Use the dark blue strips to bind the quilt edges.

5. Add a label to the back of the quilt.

Umbrella Days

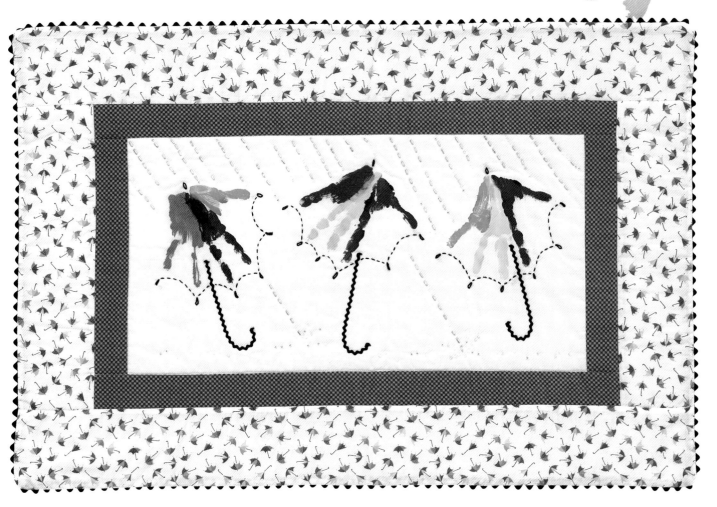

By Marcia L. Layton. Printed by 4-year-old Julia Parrino.

These bright umbrellas have opened up under a shower of sparkly beads.

Finished quilt: 30½" x 20"

MATERIALS

Yardage is based on 42"-wide fabric.

- ½ yard of white muslin for handprint panel
- ½ yard of umbrella print for outer border
- ¼ yard of blue checked fabric for inner border
- ⅞ yard of fabric for backing
- 24" x 35" piece of batting
- **Acrylic paints:** blue, green, yellow, and red
- Black embroidery floss
- ⅝ yard of black baby rickrack
- 3 yards of black medium rickrack
- White hand-quilting thread
- **Beads:** 120 *each* of clear 10/0 glass seed beads and clear bugle beads
- **Hand-sewing needles:** size 7 embroidery, size 10 milliner's
- Fabric glue

Fabric	Pieces to Cut
All measurements include ¼"-wide seam allowances.	
White muslin	1 rectangle, 14½" x 25"
Blue checked fabric	2 strips, 2" x 10½"
	2 strips, 2" x 24"
Umbrella print	2 strips, 4" x 13½"
	2 strips, 4" x 31"

MAKING THE HANDPRINT BLOCKS

Refer to "Printing the Quilt" on page 7 and "Embellishing the Quilt" on page 9. Use the quilt photo on page 33 as a placement guide for the painted features and embellishments. Use three strands of embroidery floss unless otherwise directed.

1. With straight pins, mark off the finished size of the muslin rectangle (10" x 20½") and place a pin at the horizontal and vertical centers. Using the photo on page 33 as a guide for color placement, print three evenly spaced right handprints across the bottom half of the panel. Paint each handprint with three vertical stripes of paint extending from the bottom of the palm to the fingertips. Make the hands slightly tilted with the fingers spread apart. Heat-set the prints.

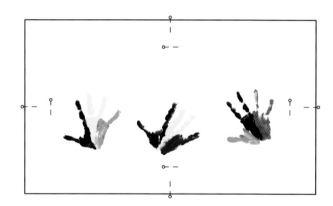

2. Rotate the panel so the handprints are upside down. Using black embroidery floss and the embroidery needle, stitch a running stitch in an arc between the fingertips of each hand. Stitch a lazy daisy stitch at each fingertip and above the palm of each handprint.

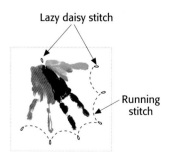

Lazy daisy stitch

Running stitch

3. Using the photo on page 33 as a guide, glue a 6" length of baby rickrack below each handprint to form an umbrella handle.

4. Trim the panel to 10½" x 21", keeping the design centered.

CONSTRUCTING THE QUILT

1. Sew the 2" x 10½" blue checked inner-border strips to the sides of the panel, and then sew the 2" x 24" blue checked inner-border strips to the top and bottom. Press the seam allowances toward the border after each addition.

2. Sew the 4" x 13½" umbrella print outer-border strips to the sides of the quilt, and then sew the 4" x 31" umbrella print outer-border strips to the top and bottom. Press the seam allowances toward the outer border after each addition.

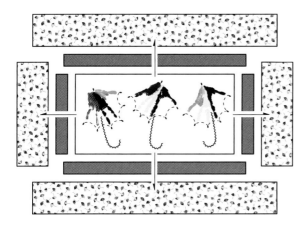

FINISHING THE QUILT

1. Referring to "Finishing with Rickrack Edging" on page 13, construct the quilt sandwich and finish the quilt with the black medium rickrack.

2. Machine quilt along the seam lines.

3. With the milliner's needle and hand-quilting thread, quilt rows of diagonal lines spaced about 1" apart from the top of the panel to the handprints. Slip a bead on each quilting stitch, randomly using seed beads and bugle beads. Allow some of the rows of beads to extend past the umbrellas to the space below them to create tiny "splashes."

4. If desired, refer to "Attaching a Hanging Sleeve" on page 14 to attach a hanging sleeve to the back of the quilt.

5. Add a label to the back of the quilt.

Special Design Tip

This motif would also be fun if the handprint umbrellas were to become beach umbrellas in a summer quilt, with quilting lines radiating from a sunshine-shaped button or appliqué and a rickrack shoreline embellished with tiny seashell-shaped buttons.

Ducks in a Row

By Marcia L. Layton. Printed by preschoolers at Play Haven Preschool.

These bright yellow ducklings are out for a stroll.

FINISHED QUILT: 29½" x 29½"

MATERIALS

Yardage is based on 42"-wide fabric.

- ⅔ yard of white muslin for handprint panels
- ⅝ yard of blue wave print for sashing and inner border*
- ⅓ yard of yellow print for outer border
- ⅓ yard of orange print for binding
- 1⅛ yards of fabric for backing
- 33½" x 33½" piece of batting
- Yellow acrylic paint
- **Dimensional fabric paints:** yellow and orange
- 6 googly eyes, 8-mm
- Fabric glue
- 1¼ yards of light green medium rickrack

Yardage is based on a directional print.

Fabric	Pieces to Cut
White muslin	2 rectangles, 10" x 21"
Blue wave print (cut on *lengthwise* grain)	2 strips, 4" x 19"
Blue wave print (cut on *crosswise* grain)	1 strip, 4" x 19"
	2 strips, 4" x 26"
Yellow print	2 strips, 2¼" x 26"
	2 strips, 2¼" x 29½"
Orange print	4 strips, 2" x 42"

All measurements include ¼"-wide seam allowances.

MAKING THE HANDPRINT PANELS

Refer to "Printing the Quilt" on page 7 and "Embellishing the Quilt" on page 9. Use the quilt photo on page 36 as a placement guide for the painted features and embellishments.

1. With straight pins, mark off the finished size of the muslin rectangle (7½" x 18½") and place a pin at the horizontal and vertical centers. Using yellow acrylic paint, print three evenly spaced right handprints across one rectangle. Each hand should be tilted to the right, with the fingers held together and the thumb extended. In the same manner, make three left handprints across the remaining rectangle. Heat-set the prints.

2. Using the quilt photo on page 36 as a guide, paint feather details on each duck with yellow dimensional paint. Use orange dimensional paint to make the bill and webbed feet for each duck.

3. Glue an 8-mm googly eye to each thumbprint.

4. Trim the handprint panels to 8" x 19", keeping the designs centered.

CONSTRUCTING THE QUILT

1. Sew a length of light green rickrack to the bottom of each panel, centering the rickrack on the ¼" seam line.

2. Join the panels with the 4" x 19" blue print crosswise-cut sashing strip. Press the seam allowances toward the sashing.

3. Sew the 4" x 19" blue print lengthwise-cut inner-border strips to the sides of the quilt, and then sew the 4" x 26" blue print inner-border strips to the top and bottom. Press the seam allowances toward the border after each addition.

4. Sew the 2¼" x 26" yellow print outer-border strips to the sides of the quilt, and then sew the 2¼" x 29½" yellow print outer-border strips to the top and bottom. Press the seam allowances toward the border after each addition.

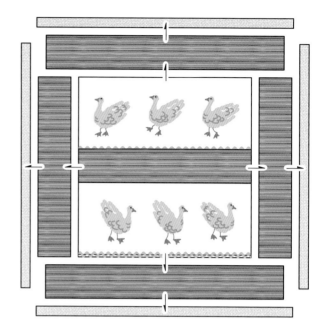

FINISHING THE QUILT

1. Referring to "Finishing with Binding" on page 11, construct the quilt sandwich, pin baste, and machine quilt along the seam lines.

2. If desired, refer to "Attaching a Hanging Sleeve" on page 14 to add a hanging sleeve to the back of the quilt.

3. Use the orange print strips to bind the quilt edges.

4. Add a label to the back of the quilt.

Special Design Tip

This quilt would be fun printed by a "family" of ducks with Mom and Dad's handprints leading and the children's handprints arranged in order of size from largest to smallest.

Strawberry Basket

By Marcia L. Layton. Printed by preschoolers at Play Haven Preschool.

These berries are big and red and oh so much fun to make!

FINISHED QUILT: 23¼" x 23¼"

MATERIALS

Yardage is based on 42"-wide fabric.

- ⅜ yard of basket-weave print for sashing, inner border, and binding
- ⅜ yard of red-and-white checked fabric for outer border
- ⅓ yard of white muslin for Handprint blocks
- ¼ yard of strawberry print for middle border
- 1 yard of fabric for backing
- 28¼" x 28¼" piece of batting
- Red acrylic paint
- 80 black 4-mm pony beads
- ⅔ yard of green jumbo rickrack
- Size 7 embroidery hand-sewing needle
- Fabric glue

All measurements include ¼"-wide seam allowances.

Fabric	Pieces to Cut
White muslin	4 squares, 7¾" x 7¾"
Basket-weave print	2 strips, 1¼" x 6¼"
	3 strips, 1¼" x 12¾"
	2 strips, 1¼" x 14¼"
	3 strips, 2" x 42"
Strawberry print	2 strips, 2¼" x 14¼"
	2 strips, 2¼" x 17¾"
Red-and-white checked fabric	2 strips, 3¼" x 17¾"
	2 strips, 3¼" x 23 ¼"

MAKING THE HANDPRINT BLOCKS

Refer to "Printing the Quilt" on page 7 and "Embellishing the Quilt" on page 9. Use the quilt photo on page 39 as a placement guide for the painted features and embellishments.

1. With red paint, print a single left handprint in the center of each muslin square. The handprint should be made with the thumb and fingers held close together. Heat-set the prints.

2. Rotate the blocks so the handprints are upside down. In a random pattern, use the embroidery needle to sew approximately 20 beads onto each of the red handprints to represent seeds. Space the beads about ¼" apart.

3. Cut four 6" lengths of rickrack. Thread the embroidery needle with green thread and tie a knot in one end of the thread. Gather each piece of rickrack by stitching into six points along one side of the trim. Pull the thread tight. This will bring the ends of the rickrack together to form a tight circle. Secure the circle by stitching through the point where you began and knotting the thread. Turn the ends under. Glue the rickrack circle in place at the top of each handprint.

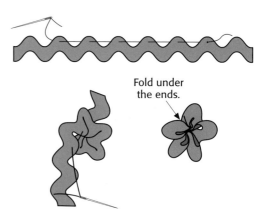

Fold under the ends.

4. Trim the blocks to 6¼" x 6¼".

CONSTRUCTING THE QUILT

1. Sew the blocks and 1¼" x 6¼" basket-weave print sashing strips into two rows as shown. Press the seam allowances toward the sashing.

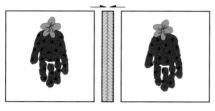

Make 2.

2. Sew the rows together, inserting a 1¼" x 12¾" basket-weave print sashing strip between them as shown. Press the seam allowances toward the sashing.

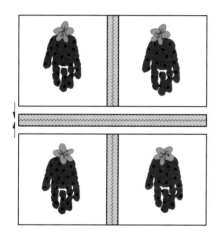

3. Sew the two remaining 1¼" x 12¾" basket-weave print inner-border strips to the sides of the quilt, and then sew the 1¼" x 14¼" basket-weave print inner-border strips to the top and bottom. Press the seam allowances toward the border after each addition.

4. Sew the 2¼" x 14¼" strawberry print middle-border strips to the sides of the quilt, and then sew the 2¼" x 17¾" strawberry print middle-border strips to the top and bottom. Press the seam allowances toward the middle borders after each addition.

5. Sew the 3¼" x 17¾" red checked outer-border strips to the sides of the quilt, and then sew the 3¼" x 23¼" red checked outer-border strips to the top and bottom. Press the seam allowances toward the outer borders after each addition.

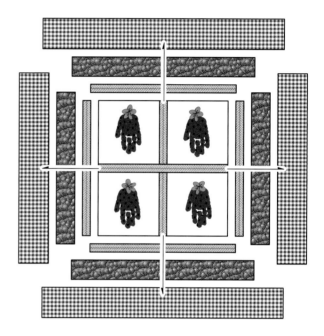

FINISHING THE QUILT

1. Referring to "Finishing with Binding" on page 11, construct the quilt sandwich, pin baste, and machine quilt along the seam lines.

2. Quilt around the strawberries. Quilt in a criss-cross pattern over the Handprint block backgrounds to give them some dimension.

3. If desired, refer to "Attaching a Hanging Sleeve" on page 14 to attach a hanging sleeve to the back of the quilt.

4. Use the basket-weave print strips to bind the quilt edges.

5. Add a label to the back of the quilt.

Undersea Fantasy

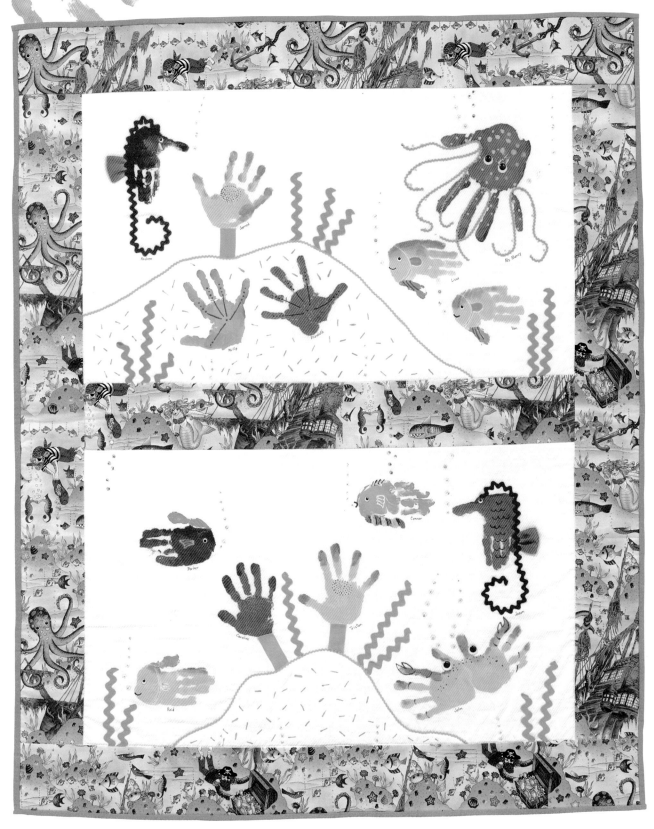

By Marcia L. Layton. Printed by the 2002–2003 class of 4-year-olds at Play Haven Preschool.

A host of sea creatures swim around pirate treasure in this bubbly undersea world.

FINISHED QUILT: 38" x 46½"

MATERIALS

Yardage is based on 42"-wide fabric.

- 1⅝ yards of sea print for sashing and border*
- 1¼ yards of white muslin for handprint panels
- ⅜ yard of turquoise fabric for binding
- 1⅝ yards of fabric for backing
- 42" x 51" piece of batting
- **Baby rickrack:** 2 yards of light green, 1½ yards of pink
- **Acrylic paints:** green, pink, yellow, orange, and dark pink
- **Jumbo rickrack:** 2 yards of light green
- **Dimensional fabric paints:** bright green, orange, dark green, dark pink, turquoise, and yellow
- **Medium rickrack:** ½ yard *each* of orange and fuchsia
- **Ribbon:** 3" *each* of 2"-wide orange satin and pink satin, ⅓ yard of 1"-wide green grosgrain
- 7 googly eyes, 8-mm; 4 googly eyes, 12-mm
- Fabric glue
- **Sequins:** approximately 90 iridescent in assorted sizes (5-, 8-, and 12-mm), approximately 50 gold 5-mm (optional)
- 10/0 glass seed beads in numbers and colors to match sequins
- Size 10 milliner's hand-sewing needle

Yardage is based on a directional print. For a non-directional print, purchase ⅝ yard.

All measurements include ¼"-wide seam allowances.	
Fabric	**Pieces to Cut**
White muslin	2 rectangles, 19½" x 32"
Sea print (cut on *crosswise* grain)	1 strip, 4½" x 30"
	2 strips, 4½" x 38"
Sea print (cut on *lengthwise* grain)*	2 strips, 4½" x 38½"
Turquoise fabric	5 strips, 2" x 42"

Cutting is based on a directional print. For a non-directional print, cut all strips on the crosswise grain.

MAKING THE HANDPRINT PANELS

Refer to "Printing the Quilt" on page 7 and "Embellishing the Quilt" on page 9. Use the quilt photo on page 42 as a placement guide for the painted features and embellishments.

1. With straight pins, mark off the finished size of each muslin rectangle (17" x 29½") and place a pin at the horizontal and vertical centers.

2. Using the photo on page 42 as a guide, glue lengths of light green baby rickrack across each panel to depict small sand hills.

Top Panel

1. On the sand hill, with the fingers spread apart, print a green handprint starfish with the right hand and a pink handprint starfish with the left hand. Then paint the right hand yellow, adding some orange shading to the fingers and thumb. Place this handprint a few inches above the hill to make a sea anemone.

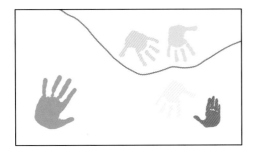

2. Rotate the panel so the image is upside down. With the fingers spread apart, print a pink handprint octopus in the lower-left corner with the left hand. In the right corner, with the right hand, print an orange handprint sea horse with the thumb extended to the side and the fingers held together.

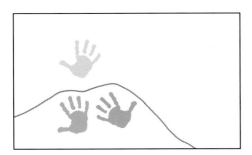

3. Rotate the panel so that the octopus is in the upper-left corner, and print two handprint fish to the right of the octopus. On the left hand, paint the thumb green and the fingers yellow with some orange shading on the side. Extend the thumbs slightly and hold the fingers together to print. Heat-set the prints.

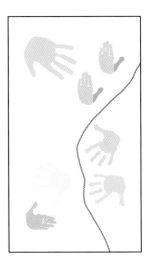

4. Rotate the panel a quarter turn to the right so that the sand hill is in an upright position. Using the quilt photo on page 42 as a guide, glue varied lengths of green jumbo rickrack to the panel in clusters to form sea grass. With bright green dimensional paint, make tiny lines all over the sand hill.

5. To finish the sea horse, glue the orange medium rickrack down the side of the orange handprint to form the back and tail. While the glue is still wet, cut and fold the 3" piece of 2"-wide orange satin ribbon in half widthwise and tuck the cut edge under the rickrack along the sea horse's back. With orange dimensional paint, make rows of scallops across the body of the sea horse. Glue an 8-mm googly eye in place at the base of the thumbprint.

6. To finish the starfish, draw lines and dots on the handprints with dimensional paint to highlight the arms. Use dark green paint on the green handprint and dark pink paint on the pink handprint.

7. To finish the sea anemone, cut and glue a length of 1"-wide green grosgrain ribbon, positioning it to extend from the base of the handprint to the sand hill and turning the raw edges under. Using turquoise dimensional paint, make a circle of dots in the top center of the palm.

8. To finish the octopus, cut four 12" lengths of pink baby rickrack. Fold each length in half, but do not crease it at the fold. With the folds close to the base of the fingers, glue the lengths in place to create eight tentacles. With yellow dimensional paint, make dots all over the handprint and down the tentacles. Glue two 12-mm googly eyes in the center of the palm.

9. To finish the fish, draw a curved line across the palm of each handprint with bright green dimensional paint to mark off the face of the fish. Draw a small fin extending back from this line toward the fingers of the handprint. With dark green dimensional paint, paint a mouth on each face and add green stripes to

the thumbprints. Glue an 8-mm eye on each fish.

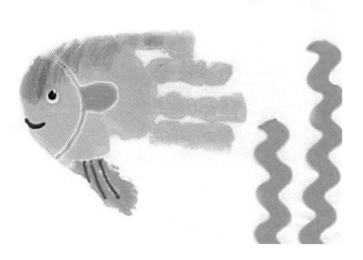

Bottom Panel

1. With the fingers and thumb of the right hand spread apart, make a sea anemone by printing a yellow handprint with orange shading just above the center of the sand hill. In the same manner, use pink with dark pink shading to make another sea anemone to the left of the first one. To make the crab, paint the right and left hands with yellow paint and shade them with orange. Place the handprints in the lower-right corner of the panel with the base of the thumbs touching and the fingers spread apart.

2. Rotate the panel so that the image is upside down and print a pink handprint sea horse in the lower-left corner with the fingers held together and the thumb out to the side.

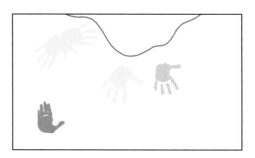

3. Rotate the panel a quarter turn to the right. Paint the thumb of the right hand green and the fingers yellow with some orange shading on the side. Extend the thumb slightly and hold the fingers together. Make a handprint fish in the lower-right corner of the panel. With the fingers of the left hand painted green and the thumb painted with pink and yellow stripes, make another fish handprint below the thumb of the sea horse handprint.

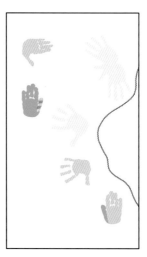

4. Rotate the panel 180° so that the sea horse handprint is in the bottom right corner. With the fingers of the left hand painted orange and the thumb painted green, print a fish in the

upper-right corner of the panel. Heat-set the prints.

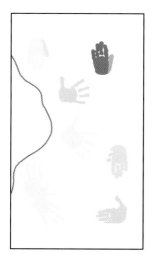

5. Refer to the instructions for the top panel to glue rickrack sea grass to the bottom panel. Finish the sea horse with fuchsia rickrack and pink ribbon; finish the sea anemones with paint and ribbon. Embellish the three fish with painted fins in a manner similar to those in the top panel, referring to the photo as needed. Add 8-mm googly eyes to the sea horse and fish.

6. Draw the features of the crab with orange dimensional paint. Glue two 12-mm googly eyes in place near the base of the thumbs of the handprint.

CONSTRUCTING THE QUILT

1. Trim each panel to 17½" x 30".

2. Sew the 4½" x 30" sea print sashing strip between the two panels. Press the seam allowances toward the sashing.

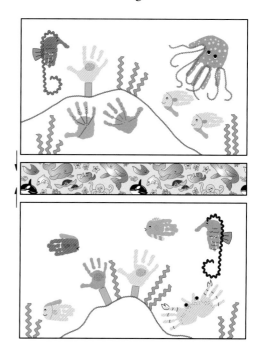

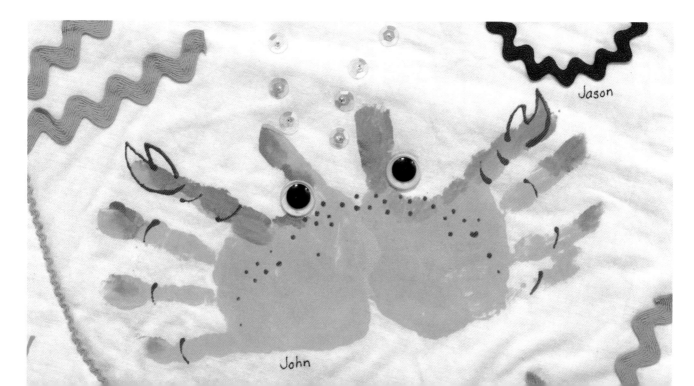

3. Sew the 4½" x 38½" sea print borders to the sides of the quilt, and then sew the 4½" x 38" sea print borders to the top and bottom. Press the seam allowances toward the border after each addition.

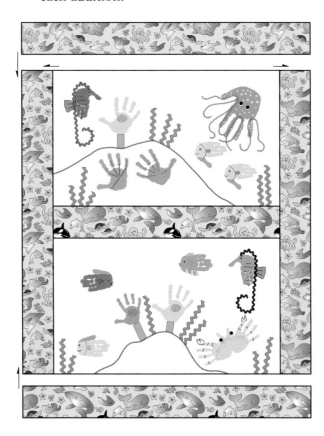

4. Referring to the photo on page 42 as a guide, use the milliner's needle to sew the assorted sizes of iridescent sequin "bubbles" with matching seed beads to the handprint panels. If the print you use for the sashing and border contains open treasure chests and bags of gold coins, randomly sew the 5-mm gold sequins with matching seed beads to some of the coins.

FINISHING THE QUILT

1. Referring to "Finishing with Binding" on page 11, construct the quilt sandwich, pin baste, and machine quilt along the seam lines. Also quilt along the rickrack lines of the sand hills on each panel.

2. If desired, refer to "Attaching a Hanging Sleeve" on page 14 to add a hanging sleeve to the back of the quilt.

3. Use the turquoise strips to bind the quilt edges.

4. Add a label to the back of the quilt.

Special Design Tip

The border print inspired all the sea creatures on these panels and influenced my choice of colors and embellishments as well. I like to match things up, but that isn't always possible or necessary. These creatures could be framed with a plain blue water print or solid and look just as enchanting.

Flamingo Fun

By Marcia L. Layton. Printed by 4-year-old Lissa Ogden.

This bright pink bird is ready to strut his stuff in the summer sunshine!

Finished quilt: 16" x 20"

MATERIALS

Yardage is based on 42"-wide fabric.

- ½ yard of white muslin for handprint panel
- ½ yard of flamingo print for border*
- ¼ yard of pink print for binding
- ⅔ yard of fabric for backing
- 20" x 24" piece of batting
- Hot pink acrylic paint
- ⅔ yard of hot pink ⅜"-wide grosgrain ribbon
- **Dimensional fabric paints:** black, hot pink, green, and light green
- Sunglasses-shaped button
- Fabric glue

*Yardage is based on a directional print. For a non-directional print, purchase ¼ yard.

All measurements include ¼"-wide seam allowances.	
Fabric	**Pieces to Cut**
White muslin	1 rectangle, 12" x 16"
Flamingo print (cut on *lengthwise* grain)*	2 strips, 3½" x 14"
Flamingo print (cut on *crosswise* grain)	2 strips, 3½" x 16"
Pink print	2 strips, 2" x 42"

*Cutting is based on a directional print. For a non-directional print, cut all strips on the crosswise grain.

MAKING THE HANDPRINT BLOCK

Refer to "Printing the Quilt" on page 7 and "Embellishing the Quilt" on page 9. Use the quilt photo on page 49 as a placement guide for the painted features and embellishments.

1. With straight pins, mark off the finished size of the muslin rectangle (9½" x 13½"). Position the rectangle so that the long sides are horizontal. Divide the finished panel area in half and pin-mark.

2. With hot pink paint, print a right handprint in the center of the left half of the panel. Print with the thumb extended to the side and the fingers pointing away from you. Heat-set the print.

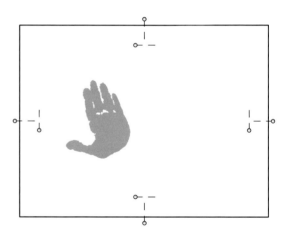

3. Rotate the panel 90° to the right so that the handprint is at the top of the panel. Cut the ribbon into two 10½" lengths. Knot each length of ribbon near its middle. Using the photo on page 49 as a guide, position one ribbon below the handprint to form one of the flamingo's legs. Glue the ribbon in place. The

bottom of the ribbon should be folded up and then down and tucked under to form the foot. Glue the second length of ribbon in place in the same manner, crossing it over the first.

4. Use black dimensional paint to draw a beak at the end of the thumbprint and hot pink dimensional paint to draw feathers on the fingerprints. With the green and light green dimensional paints, draw blades of grass near the flamingo's feet.

5. Cut the shank off the sunglasses-shaped button and glue the button in place above the thumbprint, near the flamingo's beak.

6. Trim the panel to 10" x 14".

CONSTRUCTING THE QUILT

Sew the 3½" x 14" flamingo print border strips to the sides of the quilt, and then sew the 3½" x 16" flamingo print border strips to the top and bottom. Press the seam allowances toward the border after each addition.

FINISHING THE QUILT

1. Referring to "Finishing with Binding" on page 11, construct the quilt sandwich, pin baste, and machine quilt along the seam lines.

2. If desired, refer to "Attaching a Hanging Sleeve" on page 14 to attach a hanging sleeve to the back of the quilt.

3. Use the pink strips to bind the quilt edges.

4. Add a label to the back of the quilt.

Sunshine

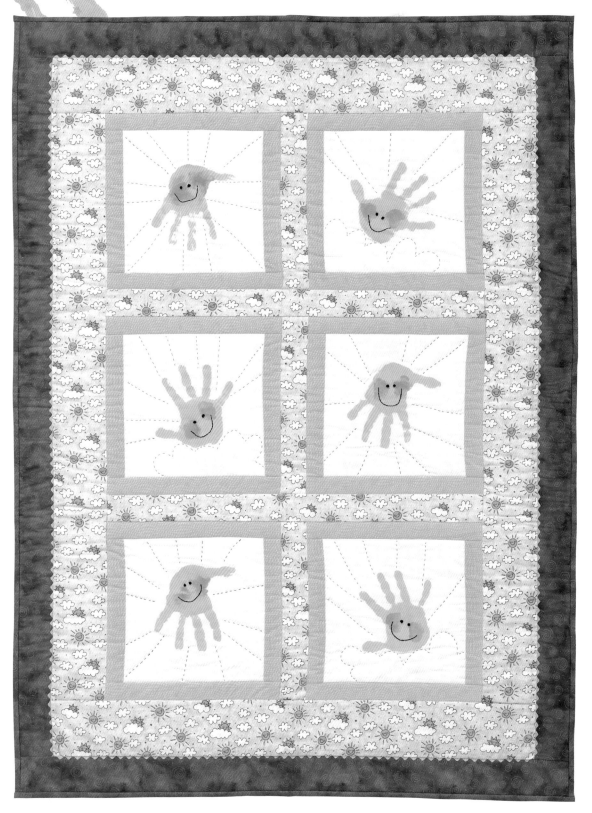

By Marcia L. Layton. Printed by 3-year-olds Gavin Smith and Danielle Wilson.

Put a little sunshine in your day with these bright yellow Handprint blocks.

FINISHED QUILT: 32½" x 44"

MATERIALS

Yardage is based on 42"-wide fabric.

- 1⅛ yards of sun print for sashing and inner border*
- ⅔ yard of white muslin for Handprint blocks
- ⅝ yard of blue print for outer border and binding
- ⅜ yard of yellow print for block borders
- 1½ yards of fabric for backing
- 37" x 48" piece of batting
- **Acrylic paints:** yellow, orange
- 12 black 4-mm pony beads
- Black embroidery floss
- 4 yards of yellow medium rickrack
- Size 7 embroidery needle

*Yardage is based on a directional print. For a non-directional print, purchase ⅔ yard.

Fabric	Pieces to Cut
White muslin	6 squares, 10½" x 10½"
Yellow print	12 strips, 1½" x 8½"
	12 strips, 1½" x 10½"
Sun print (cut on *lengthwise* grain)*	3 strips, 2" x 10½"
	2 strips, 3½" x 33½"
Sun print (cut on *crosswise* grain)	2 strips, 2" x 22"
	2 strips, 3½" x 28"
Blue print	2 strips, 2¾" x 39½"
	2 strips, 2¾" x 32½"
	4 strips, 2" x 42"

All measurements include ¼"-wide seam allowances.

*Cutting is based on a directional print. For a non-directional print, cut all strips on the crosswise grain.

MAKING THE HANDPRINT BLOCKS

Refer to "Printing the Quilt" on page 7 and "Embellishing the Quilt" on page 9. Use the quilt photo on page 52 as a placement guide for the painted features and embellishments.

1. Paint a right hand with yellow paint and add two circles of orange paint to the palm for the sun's cheeks. Spread the fingers apart and print the hand in the center of a muslin square. Repeat to make a total of six blocks. Heat-set the handprints.

2. Embellish three handprints with the fingers pointing upward and three handprints with the fingers pointing downward. To embellish each block, use the embroidery needle to sew two black beads on the palm of each hand for eyes. With three strands of black floss and the embroidery needle, backstitch a smile across the palm of each hand from the center of one cheek to the center of the other.

3. Trim the blocks to 8½" x 8½".

CONSTRUCTING THE QUILT

1. Sew the 1½" x 8½" yellow block borders to the sides of each block, and then sew the 1½" x 10½" yellow block borders to the top and bottom. Press the seam allowances toward the border after each addition.

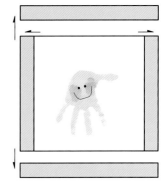

2. Using the photo on page 52 as a guide, arrange the blocks and 2" x 10½" sun print sashing strips in three rows as shown. Be sure there is one block with the fingers pointing upward and one block with the fingers pointing downward in each row. Sew the blocks and sashing strip in each row together. Press the seam allowances toward the sashing.

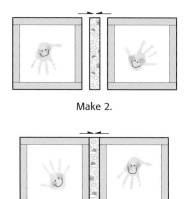

Make 2.

Make 1.

3. Join the rows, inserting a 2" x 22" sun print sashing strip between them. Press the seam allowances toward the sashing.

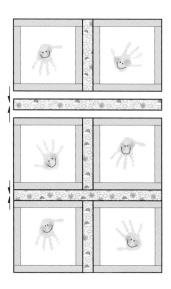

4. Sew the 3½" x 33½" sun print inner-border strips to the sides of the quilt, and then sew the 3½" x 28" sun print inner-border strips to the top and bottom. Press the seam allowances toward the border after each addition.

5. Sew the yellow rickrack to the edge of the quilt along the ¼" seam line.

6. Add the 2¾" x 39½" blue print outer-border strips to the sides of the quilt, and then sew the 2¾" x 32½" blue print outer-border strips to the top and bottom. Press the seam allowances toward the inner border after each addition. (The yellow rickrack should extend into the blue outer border on the top of the quilt.)

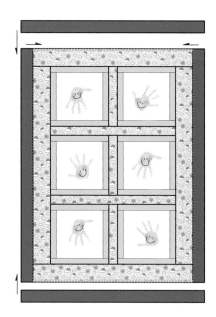

FINISHING THE QUILT

1. Referring to "Finishing with Binding" on page 11, construct the quilt sandwich, pin baste, and machine quilt along the seam lines.

2. In each block that has the fingers pointing upward, quilt a cloud below the handprint and sunshine rays above the handprint. Quilt sunshine rays all around the handprints with the fingers pointing downward.

3. If desired, refer to "Attaching a Hanging Sleeve" on page 14 to attach a hanging sleeve to the back of the quilt.

4. Use the blue print strips to bind the quilt edges.

5. Add a label to the back of the quilt.

Spider Ring

By Marcia L. Layton. Printed by 4-year-old Andrew Mathias.

These itsy-bitsy spiders are dropping in for a Halloween visit.

Finished quilt: 18" x 23½"

MATERIALS

Yardage is based on 42"-wide fabric.

- ½ yard of white muslin for handprint panel
- ¼ yard of spider print for border
- ¾ yard of fabric for backing
- 22" x 28" piece of batting
- Black acrylic paint
- ½ yard of black ⅛"-wide grosgrain ribbon
- 3 yards of black baby rickrack
- 3 pairs of 20-mm googly eyes
- Fabric glue
- 2½ yards of yellow jumbo rickrack

All measurements include ¼"-wide seam allowances.	
Fabric	**Pieces to Cut**
White muslin	1 rectangle, 14" x 19½"
Spider print	2 strips, 3½" x 12½"
	2 strips, 3½" x 24"

MAKING THE HANDPRINT PANEL

Refer to "Printing the Quilt" on page 7.

1. With straight pins, mark off the finished size of the muslin rectangle (12" x 17½"). Using black paint, print three right hands across the center of the rectangle. Stagger their placement, placing the center hand slightly above the other two. Spread the fingers apart to make the handprints. Heat-set the prints.

2. Rotate the rectangle so the handprints are upside down. Glue a length of ribbon from the top (palm) of each handprint to the top edge of the rectangle.

3. Cut 12 lengths of baby rickrack, each 8" long. For each spider's legs, glue four pieces of rickrack along the sides of the fingers, keeping the center of the pieces near the base of the fingers and extending the ends of the rickrack beyond the fingertips. This is not an exact process, and you may need to cut some of the rickrack pieces in half to better match them up to your handprints. Also, since we have five fingers, and spiders have eight legs, not all fingerprints will have a piece of rickrack on both sides.

4. Glue a pair of 20-mm googly eyes to each print on the palm area near the base of the fingers.

5. Trim the handprint panel to 12½" x 18".

CONSTRUCTING THE QUILT

1. Sew the 3½" x 12½" spider print border strips to the sides of the panel, and then sew the 3½" x 24" spider print border strips to the top and bottom. Press the seam allowances toward the border after each addition.

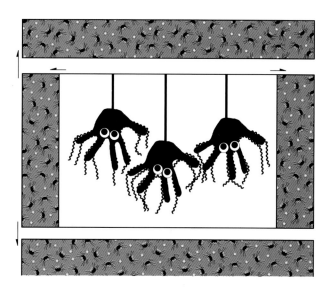

2. Sew a length of yellow rickrack to each edge of the quilt, centering it along the ¼" seam line.

FINISHING THE QUILT

1. Referring to "Finishing with Rickrack Edging" on page 13, construct the quilt sandwich, pin baste, and machine quilt along the seam lines.

2. Using the photo on page 55 as a guide, quilt a spiderweb across the background of the panel. To do this, first pick a point near the top of the panel for the center of the web. From this point, stitch radiating lines to the edges of the panel. Cross the straight lines in a circular fashion to complete the web.

3. If desired, refer to "Attaching a Hanging Sleeve" on page 14 to attach a hanging sleeve to the back of the quilt.

4. Add a label to the back of the quilt.

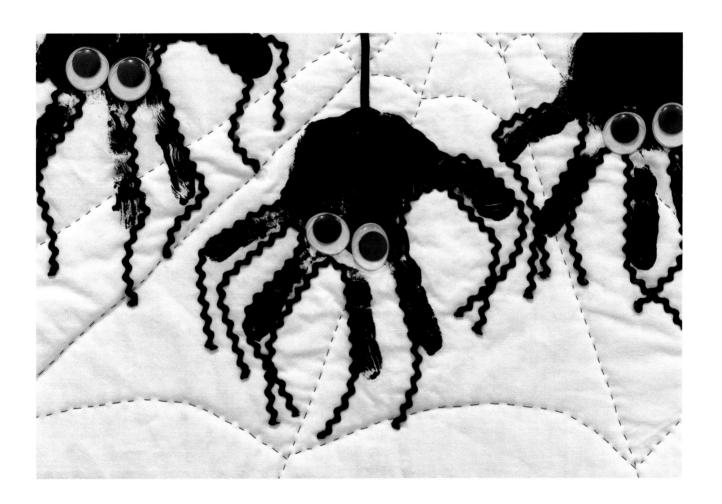

Boo!

By Marcia L. Layton. Printed by 4-year-olds Andrew Mathias,
Skylar McCain, Sarina Hunt, and Laurel Thaxton.

Spooky little ghosts peek out from the windows of this haunted quilt.

FINISHED QUILT: 29½" x 39½"

MATERIALS

Yardage is based on 42"-wide fabric.

- 1⅛ yards of Halloween print for outer border*
- ⅔ yard of black solid for Handprint blocks
- ½ yard of purple print for sashing and inner border
- ½ yard of iridescent spiderweb netting
- ⅓ yard of orange-and-blue checked fabric for binding
- 1⅜ yards of fabric for backing
- 34" x 44" piece of batting
- White acrylic paint
- **Dimensional fabric paints:** black, silver glitter
- 2½ yards of black medium rickrack
- 3¼ yards of ⅜"-wide gray satin ribbon
- Fabric glue

*Yardage is based on a directional print. For a nondirectional print, purchase ⅝ yard.

Fabric	Pieces to Cut
Black solid	6 squares, 10½" x 10½"
Purple print	3 strips, 2½" x 8½"
	2 strips, 2½" x 18½"
	2 strips, 2½" x 28½"
	2 strips, 2½" x 22½"
Halloween print (cut on *lengthwise* grain)*	2 strips, 4" x 32½"
Halloween print (cut on *crosswise* grain)	2 strips, 4" x 29½"
Orange-and-blue checked fabric	4 strips, 2" x 42"

All measurements include ¼"-wide seam allowances.

*Cutting is based on a directional print. For a nondirectional print, cut all strips on the crosswise grain.

MAKING THE HANDBLOCK PRINTS

Refer to "Printing the Quilt" on page 7 and "Embellishing the Quilt" on page 9. Use the quilt photo on page 58 as a placement guide for the painted features and embellishments.

1. With straight pins, mark off the finished size of the black squares (8" x 8"). Using white paint and holding the fingers and thumb together, print right hands in the lower-left corners of three black squares and right hands in the lower-right corners of the remaining three black squares. Heat-set the prints.

2. Rotate the squares so the handprints are upside down. Use the black dimensional paint to create a face on the palm of each handprint ghost.

3. For each square, cut a piece of spiderweb netting large enough to extend diagonally across the corner opposite the handprint. Don't worry if the piece extends beyond the square edges. The excess will be trimmed away later. Pin down the netting and glue a length of black rickrack over the diagonal edge of the netting to secure it.

4. Trim the squares to 8½" x 8½".

5. Glue lengths of gray ribbon across the vertical and horizontal centers of each square to create windowpanes.

6. With the silver glitter paint, write "BOO!" in the background of each block.

CONSTRUCTING THE QUILT

1. Sew the blocks and 2½" x 8½" purple sashing strips into three rows as shown. Press the seam allowances toward the sashing.

Make 3.

2. Sew the rows together, inserting a 2½" x 18½" purple sashing strip between each row as shown. Press the seam allowances toward the sashing.

3. Sew the 2½" x 28½" purple inner-border strips to the sides of the quilt, and then sew the 2½" x 22½" purple inner-border strips to the top and bottom. Press the seam allowances toward the border after each addition.

4. Sew the 4" x 32½" Halloween print outer-border strips to the sides of the quilt, and then sew the 4" x 29½" Halloween print outer-border strips to the top and bottom. Press the seam allowances toward the outer border after each addition.

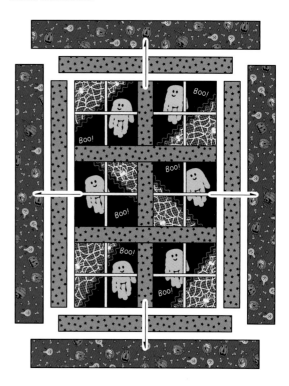

FINISHING THE QUILT

1. Referring to "Finishing with Binding" on page 11, construct the quilt sandwich, pin baste, and machine quilt along the seam lines.

2. If desired, refer to "Attaching a Hanging Sleeve" on page 14 to attach a hanging sleeve to the back of the quilt.

3. Use the orange-and-blue checked strips to bind the quilt edges.

4. Add a label to the back of the quilt.

Turkey Talk

By Marcia L. Layton. Printed by 4-year-old Melody Jay.

This handprint turkey happily celebrates the holiday because he will never be an edible part of the Thanksgiving feast!

Finished quilt: 18" x 18"

MATERIALS

Yardage is based on 42"-wide fabric.

- ⅜ yard of white muslin for Handprint block
- ⅓ yard of turkey print for outer border
- ¼ yard of corn print for flange and binding
- ¼ yard of yellow print for prairie points
- ⅛ yard of feather print for inner border
- ¾ yard of fabric for backing
- 22" x 22" piece of batting
- **Acrylic paints:** brown, yellow, orange, and red
- **Dimensional fabric paints:** yellow, orange, red, and brown
- 8-mm googly eye
- Fabric glue

All measurements include ¼"-wide seam allowances.

Fabric	Pieces to Cut
White muslin	1 square, 10½" x 10½"
Corn print	4 strips, 1¼" x 8½"
	2 strips, 2" x 42"
Feather print	2 strips, 1¾" x 8½"
	2 strips, 1¾" x 11"
Yellow print	20 squares, 3" x 3"
Turkey print	2 strips, 4" x 11"
	2 strips, 4" x 18"

MAKING THE HANDPRINT BLOCK

Refer to "Printing the Quilt" on page 7 and "Embellishing the Quilt" on page 9. Use the quilt photo on page 61 as a placement guide for the painted features and embellishments.

1. With straight pins, mark off the finished size of the muslin square (8" x 8"). Using the quilt photo as a guide, paint a right hand with brown, yellow, orange, and red acrylic paint. With brown paint, cover the thumb and most of the palm except for the lower-left corner. Paint this area yellow, orange, and red. Paint the fingers with horizontal stripes of red, orange, and yellow. With the thumb and fingers spread slightly apart, print the handprint in the center of the muslin square. With a fingertip, make a small red dot to the left of the thumbprint for the turkey's wattle. Heat-set the print.

2. Paint the turkey's features using the yellow dimensional paint for the beak and comb and the yellow, orange, and red dimensional paints for the wing and tail feather details. Draw the legs and feet with the brown dimensional paint.

3. Glue the 8-mm googly eye on the thumbprint.

4. Trim the block to 8½" x 8½".

CONSTRUCTING THE QUILT

1. Press the 1¼" x 8½" corn print flange strips in half lengthwise. Sew a strip to the sides of the block, with the folded edge of the flange

toward the center of the block and the raw edges even with the raw edges of the block. Sew the two remaining flange strips to the top and bottom of the block.

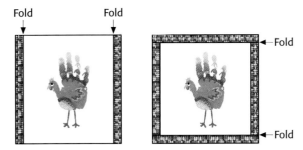

2. Sew the 1¾" x 8½" feather print inner-border strips to the sides of the block, and then sew the 1¾" x 11" feather print inner-border strips to the top and bottom. Press the seam allowances toward the border after each addition.

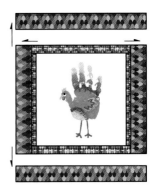

3. Fold each yellow print square in half, wrong sides together, to make a triangle. Press and fold in half again. Press once more to complete the prairie points.

Make 20.

4. With the raw edges aligned, arrange five prairie points along each edge of the block, over-

lapping them to fit. Hand baste them in place along the ¼" seam line.

5. Sew the 4" x 11" turkey print outer-border strips to the sides of the block, and then sew the 4" x 18" turkey print strips to the top and bottom. Press the seam allowances toward the inner border after each addition. The prairie points will extend into the outer border.

FINISHING THE QUILT

1. Referring to "Finishing with Binding" on page 11, construct the quilt sandwich, pin baste, and machine quilt along the seam lines.

2. If desired, refer to "Attaching a Hanging Sleeve" on page 14 to attach a hanging sleeve to the back of the quilt.

3. Bind the edges with the corn print strips.

4. Add a label to the back of the quilt.

Mittens

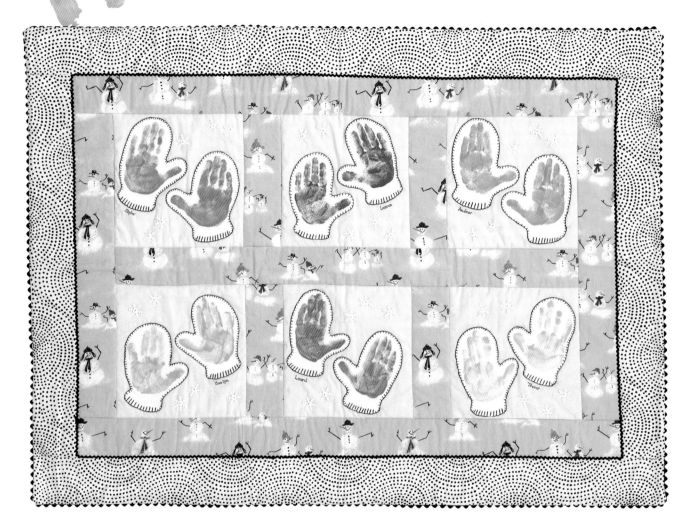

By Marcia L. Layton. Printed by 4-year-olds Skylar McCain, Lauren Pieper, Andrew Mathias, Carlyn Duke, Laurel Thaxton, and Trevor Jay at Play Haven Preschool.

Warm and fuzzy pastel handprint mittens brighten up a snowy day.

FINISHED QUILT: 41½" x 30½"

MATERIALS

Yardage is based on 42"-wide fabric.

- 1⅓ yards of black-and-white print for outer border
- 1 yard of snowman print for sashing and inner border*
- ¾ yard of pale blue solid for blocks
- Six 9" x 12" rectangles of white felt for mittens
- 1½ yards of fabric for backing
- 46" x 34" piece of batting
- **Acrylic paints:** light blue, green, lavender, orange, pink, and yellow
- Black embroidery floss
- 30 iridescent snowflake sequins
- 30 clear glass 10/0 seed beads
- 4¼ yards of black medium rickrack
- 3½ yards of black baby rickrack
- **Hand-sewing needles:** size 10 milliner's; size 7 embroidery

Yardage is based on a directional print. For a nondirectional print, purchase ½ yard.

MAKING THE HANDPRINT BLOCKS

Refer to "Printing the Quilt" on page 7 and "Embellishing the Quilt" on page 9. Use the quilt photo on page 64 as a placement guide for the painted features and embellishments. Use three strands of embroidery floss for the stitches unless otherwise directed.

All measurements include ¼"-wide seam allowances.	
Fabric	**Pieces to Cut**
Pale blue solid	6 squares, 11" x 11"
Snowman print (cut on *lengthwise* grain)*	4 strips, 3" x 9"
	2 strips, 3" x 20"
Remaining snowman print (cut on *crosswise* grain)	1 strip, 3" x 31"
	2 strips, 3" x 36"
Black-and-white print	2 strips, 3½" x 25"
	2 strips, 3½" x 42"

Cutting is based on a directional print. For a nondirectional print, cut all strips on the crosswise grain.

1. On each piece of felt, use one of the six paint colors to print a pair of right and left handprints, holding the fingers together and the thumb extended. Heat-set the handprints.

2. Refer to the photo to cut around each handprint to create the shape of a mitten.

3. With straight pins, mark off the finished size of each pale blue square (8½" x 8½"). Pin two matching mitten shapes to each pale blue square. Stitch the shapes in place using black embroidery floss and a buttonhole stitch. Make the buttonhole stitches longer and wider apart across the bottom of the mitten shapes to resemble cuffs.

4. Trim the blocks to 9" x 9", keeping the design centered.

CONSTRUCTING THE QUILT

1. Lay out the blocks and 3" x 9" snowman print sashing strips in two rows as shown. Sew the blocks and strips in each row together. Press the seam allowances toward the sashing.

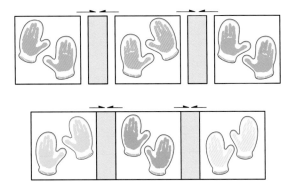

2. Sew the two rows together, inserting the 3" x 31" snowman print sashing strip between them. Press the seam allowances toward the sashing.

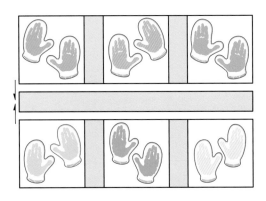

3. Sew the 3" x 20" snowman print inner-border strips to the sides of the quilt, and then sew the 3" x 36" snowman print inner-border strips to the top and bottom. Press the seam allowances toward the border after each addition.

4. Sew the 3½" x 25" black-and-white print outer-border strips to the sides of the quilt, and then sew the 3½" x 42" black-and-white print outer-border strips to the top and bottom. Press the seam allowances toward the outer border after each addition.

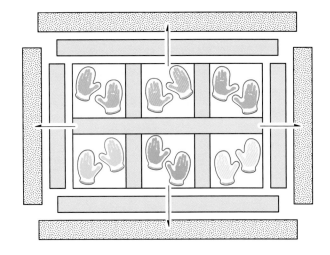

5. Attach five snowflake sequins with matching seed beads to each block in the space around the mittens.

FINISHING THE QUILT

1. Referring to "Finishing with Rickrack Edging" on page 13, construct the quilt sandwich and finish the quilt with the black medium rickrack.

2. Sew black baby rickrack on the seam line between the inner and outer borders. Machine quilt in the ditch along the remaining seam lines.

3. If desired, refer to "Attaching a Hanging Sleeve" on page 14 to attach a hanging sleeve to the back of the quilt.

4. Add a label to the back of the quilt.

Special Design Tip

I've found that painted handprints look best printed on white or off-white fabric. Other colors, even pastels, seem to distort the colors of the paint. Printing on white felt adds a nice texture to the mitten quilt and it also makes it possible to use a solid color or print as the background for the Handprint blocks.

Snow Fairy

By Marcia L. Layton. Printed by 4-year-old Reilly Goss.

This delightful Snow Fairy block combines a photo transfer image with handprints to add a little sparkle to winter.

FINISHED QUILT: 17¾" x 17¾"

MATERIALS

Yardage is based on 42"-wide fabric.

- ⅜ yard of white muslin for block
- ¼ yard of snow-fairy print for block
- ¼ yard of coordinating print for outer border
- ¼ yard of silver print for binding
- ¾ yard of fabric for backing
- 22" x 22" piece of batting
- Lavender acrylic paint
- Photo showing the neck and head of your "snow fairy" (head and neck area should measure approximately 1½" long and wide)
- Photo transfer fabric
- Scrap of fusible web
- ½ yard of white 2"-wide flat lace with scalloped edge
- Fabric glue
- ⅓ yard of ⅜"-wide silver ribbon
- Clear nylon thread
- 1 yard of silver baby rickrack
- 1½ yards of silver medium rickrack
- 5 silver 8-mm star jewels
- 9 silver snowflake sequins
- 9 clear glass 10/0 seed beads
- Silver metallic thread
- Size 10 milliner's hand-sewing needle

All measurements include ¼"-wide seam allowances.	
Fabric	**Pieces to Cut**
White muslin	1 square, 10½" x 10½"
Snow-fairy print*	2 squares, 7" x 7". Cut one square diagonally from the lower-left corner to the upper-right corner; cut the remaining square diagonally from the upper-left corner to the lower-right corner.
Coordinating print	2 strips, 3½" x 11¾"
	2 strips, 3½" x 17¾"
Silver print	2 strips, 2" x 42"

*Cutting is based on a directional print. For a non-directional print, cut the squares diagonally in either direction.

MAKING THE HANDPRINT BLOCK

Refer to "Printing the Quilt" on page 7 and "Embellishing the Quilt" on page 9. Use the quilt photo on page 67 as a placement guide for the painted features and embellishments.

1. With straight pins, mark off the finished size of the muslin square (8" x 8"). Turn the square on point. Using lavender paint, print a right and left hand in the center of the block, about 1" apart, with the thumbs pointing upward and the fingers held together and slanted to the sides. Heat-set the prints.

2. Follow the manufacturer's instructions to transfer the photo to the photo-transfer fabric. Cut out the head and neck of the desired sub-

ject from the transferred photo. Follow the manufacturer's instructions to use the fusible web to adhere the image to the muslin square between the thumbprints.

3. Cut two 8" lengths of flat lace. Hand or machine sew a line of gathering stitches along the long raw edge of one piece. Pull on the ends of the thread to gather the edge of the lace to fit around the neck of the head in the photo transfer; knot the thread ends to secure them. Tuck under the lace raw ends and glue the ruffle in place at the neck along the gathered edge and sides. Repeat to gather the remaining piece of lace, and then glue it in place under the first ruffle, positioning the piece so the first ruffle covers the gathered edge.

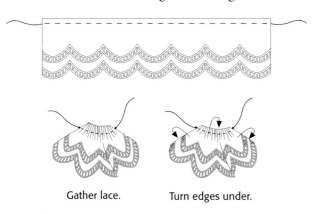

Gather lace.   Turn edges under.

4. Tie the silver ribbon in a bow and glue it in place at the top edge of the first ruffle; trim the ends as needed.

5. Trim the muslin square to 8½" x 8½", keeping the design centered.

6. Center and sew the triangles cut from one fairy print square to opposite sides of the muslin square, making sure the print will read correctly in the finished block. Press the seam allowances toward the triangles. Repeat with the remaining sides.

7. Trim the block ¼" from the muslin square points. The block should measure 11¾" square.

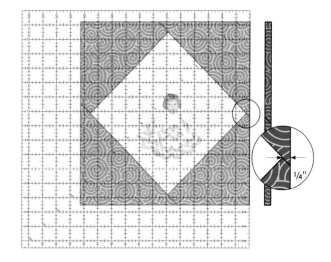

8. Using the nylon thread, sew baby rickrack on the seam line between the muslin square and corner triangles.

CONSTRUCTING THE QUILT

1. Cut a length of medium rickrack for each side of the block. Sew the pieces in place, centering them on the ¼" seam line. Be sure to taper off the rickrack ends at each corner.

2. Sew the 3½" x 11¾" coordinating print border strips to the sides of the block, and then sew the 3½" x 17¾" coordinating print border strips to the top and bottom. Press the seam allowances toward the quilt center after each addition. The points of the silver rickrack should extend into the border.

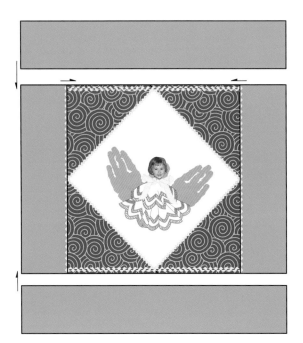

3. Glue the star jewels to the head of the photo transfer for a halo. Sew the snowflake sequins with matching seed beads to the muslin square around the snow fairy.

FINISHING THE QUILT

1. Referring to "Finishing with Binding" on page 11, construct the quilt sandwich, pin baste, and machine quilt along the seam lines.

2. Quilt around the handprints with silver metallic thread.

3. If desired, refer to "Attaching a Hanging Sleeve" on page 14 to attach a hanging sleeve to the back of the quilt.

4. Use the silver strips to bind the quilt edges.

5. Add a label to the back of the quilt.

Special Design Tip

Fairies are not just for the wintertime—there are many lovely fairy fabrics that coordinate with the flower prints of spring and summer as well. The fairy might also be used with angel fabric and given an embroidered halo and an appliquéd robe to grace a Christmas quilt.

Santa and Company

By Marcia L. Layton. Printed by 4-year-olds at Play Haven Preschool.

The handprint Santa, reindeer, and Christmas trees are fanciful additions to this holiday quilt.

FINISHED QUILT: 37½" x 37½"

MATERIALS

Yardage is based on 42"-wide fabric.

- 1 yard of white muslin for Handprint blocks
- 1 yard of Christmas print for sashing and inner border*
- ½ yard of red print for outer border
- ⅓ yard of red-and-white striped fabric for binding
- 1⅓ yards of fabric for backing
- 42" x 42" piece of batting
- **Acrylic paints:** green for Christmas trees; brown for reindeer; white, light tan, and red for Santa
- **Embroidery floss:** green, brown, and black
- **Sequins:** 28 red 8-mm round and 4 gold 12-mm star for Christmas trees, 3 black 5-mm round and 1 red 5-mm round for reindeer, 8 iridescent snowflakes for Santa
- Glass 10/0 seed beads in amount and colors to match sequins
- **⅜"-wide ribbon:** ¼ yard of brown grosgrain for Christmas trees, 2 yards of red satin for Christmas trees and reindeer
- **Googly eyes:** 4 pairs of 5-mm for reindeer, 1 pair of 8-mm for Santa
- **Pom-poms:** 8 brown, ⅜", and 4 brown, ½", for reindeer; 1 red, ⅛", and 1 white, 1", for Santa
- 24 to 28 gold 6-mm jingle bells for reindeer
- White iridescent ribbon floss for Santa's beard, eyebrows, and mustache
- Fabric glue
- **Hand-sewing needles:** size 7 embroidery; size 10 milliner's; size 22 chenille

Yardage is based on a directional print. For a nondirectional print, purchase ½ yard.

All measurements include ¼"-wide seam allowances.	
Fabric	**Pieces to Cut**
White muslin	9 squares, 10½" x 10½"
Christmas print (cut on *lengthwise* grain)*	2 strips, 2½" x 28½"
	6 strips, 2½" x 8½"
Christmas print (cut on *crosswise* grain)	2 strips, 2½" x 28½"
	2 strips, 2½" x 32½"
Red print	2 strips, 3" x 32½"
	2 strips, 3" x 37½"
Red-and-white striped	4 strips, 2" x 42"
Cutting is based on a directional print. For a nondirectional print, cut all strips on the crosswise grain.	

MAKING THE HANDPRINT BLOCKS

Refer to "Printing the Quilt" on page 7 and "Embellishing the Quilt" on page 9. Use the quilt photo on page 71 as a placement guide for the painted features and embellishments. For the embroidered details, use three strands of floss and the embroidery needle unless otherwise indicated. Attach the sequins and beads using matching all-purpose thread and the milliner's needle.

Christmas Trees

1. With green paint, print a right hand in the center of four muslin squares. Print the hand with all the fingers held closely together. Heat-set the prints.

2. Using green floss, embellish each handprint with six sets of three lazy daisy stitches placed randomly over the handprint. Attach seven red 8-mm round sequins with a matching seed bead in the spaces between the stitches. Sew a 12-mm gold star with a matching seed bead to the top of each handprint.

3. Glue a 1¼" piece of brown ribbon at the bottom of each handprint for the tree trunk. Turn under the bottom edge of the ribbon so that it won't fray. Tie a 12" length of red ribbon into a bow and glue it to the top of the brown ribbon where it meets the handprint; trim the ends as needed.

Reindeer

1. With brown paint, print a left hand in the center of two muslin squares. Spread all the fingers apart for each print. Repeat this step with the right hand on two more squares. Heat-set the prints.

2. Rotate the squares so the handprints are upside down. With brown floss, chain stitch two antlers that extend upward from each thumbprint. Glue two 5-mm googly eyes to each thumbprint. Sew a black 5-mm sequin and matching seed bead to the tip of three thumbprints and a red 5-mm sequin and matching seed bead to the remaining thumbprint. Glue two ⅜" brown pom-poms above the eyes near the antlers for ears. Glue one ½" brown pompom to the other side of each palm for a tail. With black floss, satin stitch hooves on the tips of the fingerprints.

3. Glue a length of red ribbon across each palm, carefully turning under both ends. Sew six or seven evenly spaced jingle bells to the ribbon.

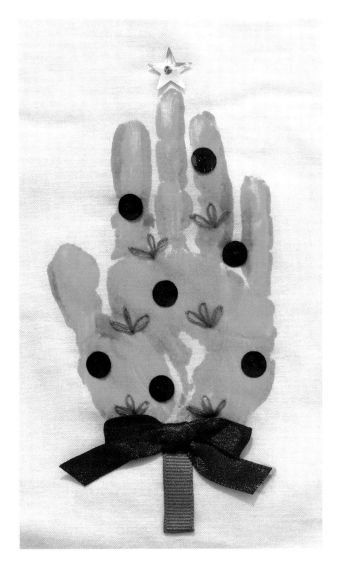

Santa

1. In the center of the remaining square, use the right hand to print a Santa face. Paint the fingers white and the top half of the palm light tan. Paint a white stripe across the center of the palm where it meets the thumb. Paint the bottom of the palm and the thumb red. Point the fingers away from you and extend the thumb to the side. Heat-set the print.

2. Rotate the square so the handprint is upside down. Using the chenille needle, one strand of white iridescent ribbon floss, and a running stitch, stitch swirls across the white areas of the handprint for the beard and fur trim on Santa's cap.

3. Glue the red ⅛" pom-pom in the center of the face. Glue the two 8-mm googly eyes slightly above and to each side of the pom-pom. With white iridescent ribbon floss and a backstitch, stitch the eyebrows and mustache.

4. Glue the white 1" pom-pom to the tip of the thumbprint. Sew the snowflake sequins with a matching seed bead to the background around Santa, referring to the photo if necessary.

CONSTRUCTING THE QUILT

1. Trim the blocks to 8½" x 8½"

2. Using the photo on page 71 as a guide, arrange the blocks and 2½" x 8½" Christmas print sashing strips into three rows as shown. Sew the blocks and sashing strips in each row together. Press the seam allowances toward the sashing.

3. Join the rows, inserting a 2½" x 28½" cross-wise-cut Christmas print sashing strip between them. Press the seam allowances toward the sashing.

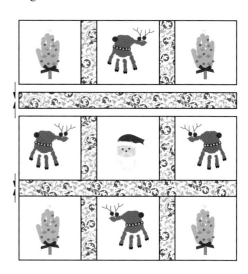

4. Sew the 2½" x 28½" lengthwise-cut Christmas print inner-border strips to the sides of the quilt, and then sew the 2½" x 32½" Christmas print inner-border strips to the top and bottom. Press the seam allowances toward the border after each addition.

5. Sew the 3" x 32½" red print outer-border strips to the sides of the quilt, and then sew the 3" x 37½" red print outer-border strips to the top and bottom. Press the seam allowances toward the outer-border strips after each addition.

FINISHING THE QUILT

1. Referring to "Finishing with Binding" on page 11, construct the quilt sandwich, pin baste, and machine quilt along the seam lines.

2. If desired, refer to "Attaching a Hanging Sleeve" on page 14 to add a hanging sleeve to the back of the quilt.

3. Use the red-and-white strips to bind the quilt edges.

4. Add a label to the back of the quilt.

HANDPRINT QUILT GALLERY

Matching Mittens

(above left) by Marcia L. Layton, 45¼" x 22½". Printed by 4-year-olds Gino Jurado, Andrew Mathias, Trevor Jay, and Corey Khaw. Colorful mittens are printed on felt as in "Mittens" on page 64 and hung from rickrack cords.

Mitten and Christmas Tree Ornaments

(above) by Marcia L. Layton. The mittens were printed by 4-year-old Melody Jay, and the tree was printed by 4-year-old Alexa Croup. The handprints were printed on white felt, cut into the desired shape, and appliquéd to a piece of red felt that was then cut slightly larger than the handprint shape. Then the ornaments were embellished.

Northwoods Friends

(left) by Marcia L. Layton, 46½" x 66½". Printed by 4-year-olds Andrew Mathias, Grey Young, and Samantha Kaltenbacher at Play Haven Preschool. Combine the reindeer handprints used in "Santa and Company" on page 71 with a classic Log Cabin block assembly, and you've got the perfect quilt for the outdoor lover.

Little Black Bears

(right) by Marcia L. Layton, 27½" x 27½". Printed by 4-year-olds Jack Casey and Laura Smith. Turn the reindeer from "Santa and Company" on page 71 into bears by using a little black paint.

A Mother's Guiding Hands

(below) by Betty Holroyd, 16½" x 14". Printed by 6-week-old Emma Holroyd and her mother, Lesley Holroyd. Find instructions for the heart design in "Calendar Kids" on page 19.

Ladybug, Ladybug

(below right) by Marcia L. Layton, 15¼" x 22". Printed by 2-year-old Carson Hales. These ladybugs are adapted from the "Calendar Kids" Ladybug block on page 22.

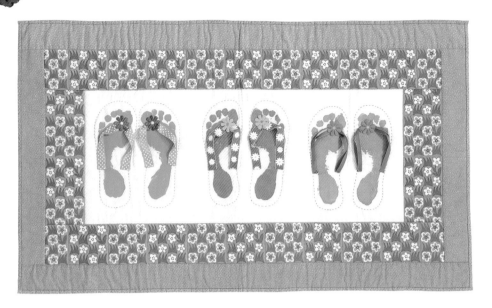

Melissa's Flip-Flops
*(left) by Marcia L. Layton, 45½" x 26¼".
Printed by Melissa Layton. These fun
shoes are perfect for a Florida girl. The
flip-flop design is featured in "Calendar
Kids" on page 23.*

Emily's Birthday Quilt
*(below left) by Maureen Stumme,
45" x 60". Printed by Emily Stumme and
her friends, Millersville, Maryland. Emily
invited friends to a pool party for her 12th
birthday, where they printed their feet and
signed their names to make the blocks for
this quilt.*

Sea Horses
*(below) by Marcia L. Layton, 30" x 23½".
Printed by 4-year-old Sophie Abel.
Instructions for making these little
sea horses can be found in "Undersea
Fantasy" on page 42.*

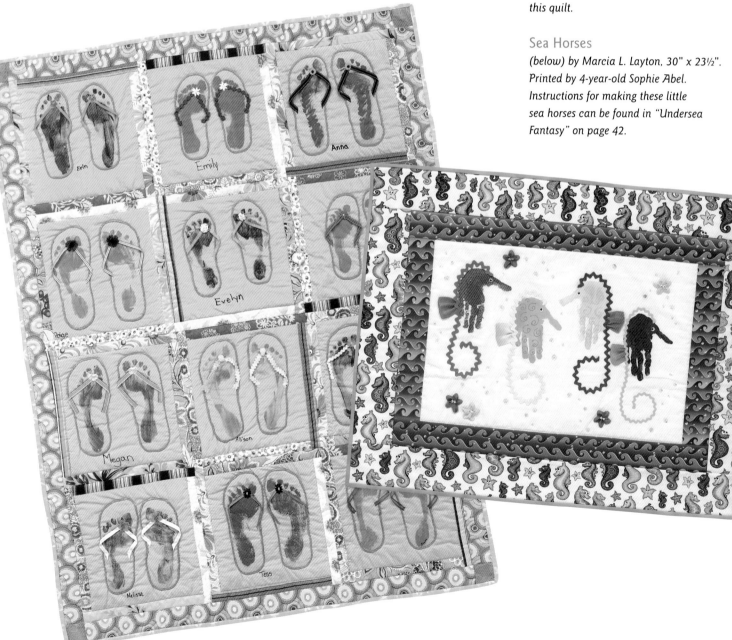

Flamingos with Leis

(above left) by Marcia L. Layton, 27½" x 24½". Printed by 4-year-old Caton Gonzalez. These flamingos, like the one in "Flamingo Fun" on page 49, are ready for a day in the sun.

Flamingo Dance

(above) by Marcia L. Layton, 32½" x 31½". Printed by Melissa Layton and Toby Fifer. This wall hanging adds handprint palm trees to the tropical scene.

Flamingo Fandango

(center left) by Marcia L. Layton, 28½" x 24½". Printed by Lauren Pieper, Lissa Ogden, Gavin Smith, and Danielle Wilson. The fabric inspired the vivid colors of these bright flamingos.

Five Little Jack-o'-Lanterns

(left) by Marcia L. Layton, 28¼" x 19". Printed by 4-year-olds at Play Haven Preschool. These happy jack-o'-lanterns are perched on a ribbon fence. The handprint design is from "Calendar Kids" on page 24.

ABOUT THE AUTHOR

Marcia L. Layton resides in Tampa, Florida, with her husband, Steve, their youngest daughter, Carrie, and three cats. Marcia has been a pre-K teacher and the assistant director of Play Haven Preschool in Tampa for the past 23 years. Inheriting a love of sewing from her grandmother and mother, Marcia has always enjoyed experimenting with all kinds of arts and crafts, from painting to smocking to embroidery, and most recently, to quilting. She started making handprint quilts for the preschool about eight years ago, and some of those quilt designs are featured in her first book, *Handprint Quilts: Creating Children's Keepsakes with Paint and Fabric* (Martingale and Company, 2003). Marcia continues to paint little hands, and she also enjoys teaching her handprint techniques to adults, all the while having fun and learning more about the world of quilting.